CONVERSATION INNOVATION

A Corporate Fable on
Leadership, Coaching, and the Power of Conversations

David G. Henkin

Published by
Transformation Press
Philadelphia, PA 19107

Book design by Doug Davala

International Standard Book Number (ISBN)
ISBN–13: 978-0-9789314-0-7
ISBN–10: 0-9789314-0-8

Printed in the United States of America

First Edition

*This book is dedicated to all those who care
as much about being their best person
as being successful—*

and to Robin Samantha.

Table of Contents

PROLOGUE

ANYTHING IS POSSIBLE

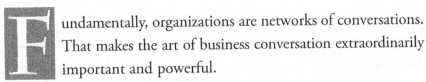undamentally, organizations are networks of conversations. That makes the art of business conversation extraordinarily important and powerful.

From a quick email exchange to a board of directors meeting, conversation is the means by which businesses forge human relationships, and make those relationships meaningful. Conversation, therefore, is a critical key to making progress and getting things done. Conversation unlocks possibilities. It enables us to do what at one time might have seemed impossible.

The story of the Tower of Babel is an illustrative case study. The book of Genesis describes an era when "the whole earth was of one language and of one speech." Unified by their common tongue, the people of the day could work cooperatively, productively. No task was too great. No challenge was insurmountable. Anything was possible.

The people built a great city, Babylon. And as a centerpiece, they set about constructing a tower so tall that its top would crest into heaven.

Genesis tells us that God saw this effort as a misguided example of human hubris, and decided to derail it with a little divine intervention. His approach was straightforward: to "confound their language, that they may not understand one another's speech." The effect was immediate, and devastating. Human speech "confounded" into babble. The one nation of man became a potpourri of different peoples. No longer a key to cooperation, language was suddenly a significant barrier. The Tower of Babel still stands—metaphorically—as a symbol of the confusion implicit in a polyglot world.

Today, the world speaks in some 1500 languages. The United Nations recognizes no fewer than five official languages. Differences in language can be a very real and powerful obstacle to communication. But conversations between people are also affected by other barriers.

In the workplace, for example, sometimes it seems as if we're reduced to a level of babble as we scramble to understand one another, explore collective possibilities, and agree to courses of action. We strain to make ourselves understood. We struggle to understand others. Working hard to define and agree to agendas, assignments, timetables, and deliverables, we often seem to talk past or around each other, failing to communicate well, if in fact we communicate at all. In other words, all too often business conversations are reduced to babble. Each of us can probably think of a project that was hampered by poor communication—by bad conversations, if you will.

Outside work, we might have similar frustrations in conversations intended to clarify agreements with spouses, for example, or to get our children to comply with our directions.

Nonetheless, we carry on to the next conversation, and the next, and the one after that. Why?

In business we carry on because, imperfect as it is, conversation is the currency through which we do our work. As we interact all day long with bosses, employees, coworkers, clients, customers, and suppliers, conversations are the way we conduct business. What we accomplish starts with and is sustained by a series of conversations.

Conversations, moreover, nurture the stories and narratives that are often the undeclared background of everyday dialogue. Those stories reflect and embody the culture of organizations. They provide powerful contexts for meaning, shaping what people see as what is possible for individuals, teams, and the organization as a whole.

In this context, the capability to nurture and manage quality conversations—and to harvest their outcomes—is a truly powerful business tool. Managing conversations well is a means to bring out our best qualities as leaders and coaches, and to bring out the best capabilities in employees and teams.

Thus, an employee's ability to communicate effectively—to maintain an ongoing series of successful conversations with a wide range of stakeholders—is crucial to his or her success. Similarly, the ability of employees as a group to have successful conversations is crucial to a business's success. In this context, therefore, it is just as important that a company monitor, manage, and improve conversational skills and capabilities as it is, for example, to manage information technology.

Nonetheless, workplace communication remains difficult to measure, and perhaps even more difficult to improve. Remarkably, while we have access to an abundance of models that help us assess and manage such critical functions as IT, project management, and process management, parallel systems or structures for systemically measuring and managing a firm's communication and conversational capabilities remain elusive. And similarly, while we spend billions of dollars on such critical assets as network infrastructures and computing resources, and invest heavily in training programs from Six Sigma to Customer Relationship Management, we do not make a similar investment in conversation.

As an antidote to the downside risks of "confounded" speech, this book proposes a model, based on ontological coaching, to measure, manage, and improve conversational communication capability in a systemic, repeatable manner. Set in a real-life context, the book is arranged into four parts: *Part One – Leaving the Comfort Zone* focuses on awareness and motivation; *Part Two – On the Runway* assesses actions, reactions, and lack-of-actions; *Part Three – Taking Flight* investigates applications and implications; and *Appendix – Methods* presents models and methodologies.

Fundamentally, this book is about ways to make conversational interactions, especially in business, as meaningful and as powerful as possible. Full of models and examples, the book can guide you in improving your own workplace conversation skills. My hope is that it will provide some take-away lessons that will enrich your own conversations, and help alleviate the frustrations and limitations of "babble."

PART ONE

LEAVING THE COMFORT ZONE

The thing that is really hard, and really amazing, is giving up on being perfect and beginning the work of becoming yourself.

—Anna Quindlen

Fear is the main source of superstition, and one of the main sources of cruelty. To conquer fear is the beginning of wisdom.

—Bertrand Russell

CHAPTER ONE

DIVERSITY DAY

Justine Fullerton took a long, deep breath and walked purposefully into the lobby of the Crown Plaza hotel. She was a little nervous. Managers at Standard Products, Inc. were required to attend diversity seminars as part of their professional development. But as a fairly new manager at SPI, Justine was new to the experience, and she wasn't sure what to expect. To help her navigate the program and get the most value from it, she had asked Nick Smith, a more senior colleague, to accompany her.

As she waited for Nick in the lobby, Justine idly reviewed the seminar materials. Her mind drifted back to the office. She found herself replaying a series of conversations with coworkers who had been surprised when she was recently promoted to manager. While people were polite, everyone seemed to note that more tenured leaders had been passed over when she got the nod. And Justine caught wind of some rumors that the CEO had played a role in her promotion. Preoccupied, Justine was startled when Nick arrived and greeted her with a booming "Good morning!"

Chatting as they joined a slow-moving mass of people in the crowded atrium, they snaked their way toward the hotel ballroom where the seminar would kick off. Inside the ornate hall, they found rows of tables neatly arranged classroom-style. A pad of paper and freshly sharpened pencils marked each person's place. Justine and Nick found seats near the front.

"I certainly hope we don't have to do a role-play," Nick said, studying the room for potential partners. Having been a manager for more than a few years, Nick had attended his share of mandatory trainings. "I've been to a bunch of these and I get why we're sent here," he said, "but the least they can do is make it easy on us."

Recruited from a competitor, Nick was a rising star at SPI. He had a record of delivering "on plan" both individually and as manager of his team, and was known for spearheading technical innovations that kept him in senior management's eye.

Justine's rise to manager had come less than a year ago, arguably ahead of schedule, and without the fanfare that accompanied Nick's rise. While she lacked the technical depth of her more senior peers, she seemed to connect with people and worked to get the most out of her relationships with colleagues.

On her office wall, Justine kept a diagram of three overlapping circles. The first was labeled "what you know." A larger circle was marked "what you know you don't know." The largest circle was labeled "what you don't know you don't know." Justine used the diagram as something of a roadmap, and referred to it often.

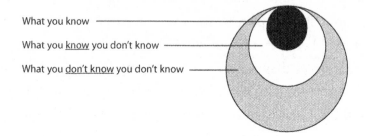

When given tough assignments, Justine typically took time to find the right resources to help her. She often sought to tackle performance improvement not so much by increasing what she knew, but by increasing her team's ability to use what others knew. Well-intentioned,

CONVERSATION INNOVATION

legitimate, and effective, that approach nonetheless often created awkward exchanges between Justine and her peers, and even with some former coworkers.

Waiting for the seminar to start, Justine noted that the last session of the day was on coaching. While she knew little of coaching per se, she had heard colleagues and others use the term many times, and she was keenly interested in knowing more about it. Her interest might also have had something to do with the fact that she was an avid sports fan and an accomplished, highly competitive volleyball player.

"Hey, did you see this session on coaching at four o'clock?" she asked Nick. Her co-worker was scanning the room for colleagues he wanted to catch at coffee breaks, and answered distractedly.

"I saw a guy do that a year or two ago. Didn't get it, but I guess that kind of stuff is still making the rounds."

They both settled in for the morning session, one quietly holding her excitement, the other quietly pacing his patience.

By late afternoon, as they waited for the coaching session to begin, Nick and Justine felt drained. The day's speakers had been engaging, and many of the sessions had been interactive and fun, yet the two colleagues were feeling the kind of fatigue that comes from sitting in a meeting all day. Justine found a fresh page in her notebook while Nick stretched and gazed out the window. Neither noticed as Victor Jamison strode to the front of the room.

Victor Jamison had been a successful high-level executive at a prominent regional company. After his kids started college, he decided to move away from traditional managerial roles to help executives find ways to be more successful.

"What is coaching?" Victor said, writing the question on the flip chart. The room quieted. People fidgeted. Nobody ventured a response.

"Maybe let's start with what coaching is not," Victor offered. "Who has ever coached a sports team?"

Many hands shot up. "Is it therapy?" he asked. Shaking heads answered no. "Is it consulting? Is it training?" Again, shaking heads.

"It's teaching," replied a gentleman in the front row. "I teach my 4th grade basketball team as part of coaching them..." and with that the discussion began in earnest.

Before long, the seminar participants had generated a long list of defining factors:

Coaching
- Occurs over time
- Operates from a client-initiated agenda
- Is based on a designed alliance
- Fosters discovery and self-learning
- Builds awareness and responsibility
- Is proactive and responsive
- Includes planning and goal setting
- Holds the client accountable
- Addresses attitude, mind set, and behavior
- Produces positive outcomes

"Coaching is a professional relationship," Victor summarized, "that enhances the client's ability to effectively focus on learning, make changes, achieve desired goals, and experience fulfillment." Attendees nodded in agreement.

By that time, the session was nearly over. To help close the day Jamison told the group he wanted to end with a parable.

The Moneylender and the Pebble

Many years ago in a small village, a farmer had the misfortune of owing a large sum of money to a village moneylender. The money-lender, who was old and ugly, fancied the farmer's beautiful daughter. So he proposed a bargain.

He said he would forgo the farmer's debt if he could marry his daughter. Both the farmer and his daughter were horrified by the proposal. So the cunning moneylender suggested that they let providence decide the matter.

He told them that he would put a black pebble and a white pebble into an empty money bag. Then the girl would have to pick one pebble from the bag.

If she picked the black pebble, she would become his wife and her father's debt would be forgiven. If she picked the white pebble she need not marry him and her father's debt would still be forgiven. But if she refused to pick a pebble, her father would be thrown into jail.

They were standing on a pebble-strewn path in the farmer's field. As they talked, the moneylender bent over to pick up two pebbles. As he picked them up, the sharp-eyed girl noticed that he had picked up two black pebbles and put them into the bag. He then asked the girl to pick a pebble from the bag.

"Now, imagine that you were standing in the field," Victor posed to the group. "What would you have done if you were the girl? If you had to advise her, what would you have told her?

"Conventional analysis would produce three possibilities:

1) The girl should refuse to take a pebble.

2) The girl should show that there were two black pebbles in the bag and expose the moneylender as a cheat.

3) The girl should pick a black pebble and sacrifice herself in order to save her father from his debt and imprisonment.

"Take a moment to ponder the story," Victor continued. "This story is used with the hope that it will make us appreciate the difference between systemic and logical thinking. The girl's dilemma cannot be solved with traditional logical thinking. Think of the consequences if she chooses one of the logical answers. What would you recommend that the girl do?

Victor paused. "Well, here is what she did:

> The girl put her hand into the moneybag and drew out a pebble. Without looking at it, she fumbled and let it fall onto the pebble-strewn path where it immediately became lost among all the other pebbles.
>
> "Oh, how clumsy of me," she said. "But never mind, if you look into the bag for the one that is left, you will be able to tell which pebble I picked."
>
> Since the remaining pebble is black, it must be assumed that she had picked the white one. And since the moneylender dared not admit his dishonesty, the girl changed what seemed an impossible situation into an extremely advantageous one.

"All simple and complex problems do have a solution," Victor stated. "But before taking action, we need to explore all possibilities.

"How would you have coached the girl or her father? How many situations are you faced with where the possibilities in front of you represent a limited few—at the office or at home?"

As the session on coaching ended, Justine felt exhilarated. What Jamison had to say answered many questions she had—and raised many new ones. She rushed to catch the speaker before he left the room. She waved goodbye to Nick, who was already halfway to the exit.

A crowd swarmed around Victor Jamison, who graciously answered questions even as a staff person tried to help him leave in time to catch a plane. Justine was able to grab his business card before they were both swept out into the hotel lobby and back into the bustling world.

CHAPTER TWO

BUSINESS AS USUAL

ounded 35 years ago, Standard Products, Inc. had expanded steadily over the years. Its staff had grown from just a few people to a few thousand, and the company now boasted more than a hundred locations around the country.

SPI's structure was fairly typical. It was led by a chief executive officer who also served as president, and who reported to a board of directors. The CEO had a staff of vice presidents with responsibility for functional and customer-aligned business units. Each VP was in charge of managers who supported the business units. Each manager directed a team of individual contributors, personnel focused on delivering tasks rather than managing people.

Most employees thought SPI was a nice place to work. In addition to taking annual employee satisfaction surveys seriously, the management team supported open-door policies, training and development programs, and promoted good employee relations. As the company grew, SPI worked hard to maintain a corporate culture of customer focus, employee satisfaction, and mutual respect.

Dragging along some reluctant old-timers, the company used improvement programs like Six Sigma and Lean to drive greater efficiency. Initial skepticism about a company-wide shift of employees to more value-added, service-oriented roles evaporated when that approach proved to be integral to the company's success. Similarly, criticism of the company's significant investment in technology quieted quickly when it began to show results.

As it grew, SPI worked with outside consultants to develop

business dashboards and process maps. In addition to supporting specific initiatives, these were intended to sustain the kind of transparency that the company had enjoyed when it was a smaller team working on one floor, even while SPI opened more physical locations and increased staff FTEs. The dashboards were prominently displayed at each department's "Vital Information Post" (or "VIP") area and were updated regularly.

Justine passed by her unit's dashboard as she hurried into her office the morning after the diversity seminar. The blinking red light on her phone told her she had voicemail, but she chose to ignore that for now. Taking off her coat, she glanced at her daily schedule, resisting a strong urge to instead open her binder from the previous day's workshop. Her thoughts began to focus on the day ahead as she grabbed her portfolio and headed down the hallway. Ducking into the kitchenette, Justine found Nick pouring himself a cup of coffee.

"Hey, what did you think of yesterday's seminar?" she asked.

"Hey Justine, how are you?" Nick started, acknowledging passersby with a slight head nod. "You know, the only thing I really remember from yesterday was that rough morning traffic," Nick said. "And the fact that I got home in time to actually help my wife rehearse for the play she's in."

"What did you think of the final session on coaching" she asked, hoping he would share even some of her energy for it.

"I didn't really get it," Nick said. "I mean, I get the whiteboard stuff and the basketball team thing, but that whole bit on problems and possibilities was way out. To be honest, I was happy to get home at a decent hour!" Nick smiled and set off down the corridor.

Justine couldn't help but feel a bit crushed. She could still hear Victor Jamison telling the story of the pebbles. For Justine, that parable was as clear a lesson as could be about the limitations most people—including herself—usually place on their experiences. Justine wondered why Nick didn't share her excitement about Jamison's insight: that people tend to focus on problems and on choosing options rather than thinking meaningfully about new possibilities.

Walking slowly back to her office, Justine passed walls decorated with technical diagrams, schematics, and process flows. A poster with a picture of a mountain advocated better customer commitment. Business dashboards outlined important department drivers and deadlines, underscoring corporate goals.

Wondering if Nick's impressions about the seminar were right, Justine recalled conversations she'd been part of recently—a typical daily meeting about customer interactions, random discussions with her team and peers, recruiting interviews, even the Town Hall-style meeting her division conducted a few weeks back. All of those meetings, Justine reflected, were about addressing challenges, improving things, taking action, and directing people. And yet she couldn't help but feel that something was missing from those discussions.

Still, operations at SPI seemed to be running productively. As she prepared to step into a meeting with her staff, Justine wondered if there was something wrong with *her*.

CHAPTER THREE

CRISIS AND OPPORTUNITY

J ustine's team consisted of three senior project managers—at SPI they were called "leads"—each of whom worked both with other internal employees and a host of external entities. Each lead worked with internal product and service managers as well as customer reps in the field. They relied on one another when larger customers were involved, and when multiple products or services were required. Nick and Justine's teams performed similar business functions for different geographical territories.

Justine's most tenured lead was Lester Fowler. Les had been at SPI almost 14 years. Before that, Les had worked in a similar capacity at a large technology company. He was the most technically savvy member of his team. In fact, employees from other departments often sought Les out for product guidance and direction. An engineer by training, he considered himself an "old-timer," even though other employees had longer tenures. Les worked expeditiously, with a very professional manner, consistently maintaining a level of quality exceeding that of most of his peers.

Fran Dunn was a 5-year veteran of SPI, coming to the company from a job in the public sector. A hard worker, she dedicated herself as much to serving colleagues and customers as she did to task work. Diligent, thorough, even meticulous, Fran truly cared about her work, and it showed in the level of effort she expended and the outputs she produced. From the start of her tenure at SPI, Fran had volunteered to represent her unit on corporate initiatives, began to network outside her team, and learned not only SPI's business but that of its competitors and the industry as well.

Matt Holmes was the most recent hire onto Justine's team, and her first "official" hire as a new manager. Eager to make her first hire a success, Justine had participated intently throughout the recruiting process with human resources, interviewing six candidates for her single opening. Matt was a recent college graduate who came directly from a brief stint as a sales rep for a large industrial manufacturer. He was bright, articulate, patient, and showed a high degree of enthusiasm during the interview process. He had clearly done his homework prior to his interviews, and asked interesting questions about the company, the team, customers, and products. Justine believed that Matt's skills and enthusiasm would bring important new perspectives to her team.

Meeting rooms at SPI were fairly attractive, for corporate offices. Many had windows and most were decorated with corporate posters, motivational messages and the like. Justine's team was in the process of sitting down as she entered the room. They quickly took their seats and watched her as she sat and opened her notebook.

As she settled into her seat, Justine felt that a familiar ritual was about to unfold. She had been conducting these early-week meetings to help her team get on the same page with regard to work-in-progress and priorities, and to help foster communication. It was clear not everyone enjoyed being pulled away from work, but Justine thought it would prove worthwhile to spend more time together as a team. She started the meeting with a casual question.

"So, I haven't seen you-all yet this week. How were your weekends?"

Lester looked away, turning his chair left and right impatiently. Matt sat quietly, alternately looking at Justine and his folder of notes. Fran began telling the others about a movie she saw on Saturday.

Before the meeting went too far off track, Justine broke in during one of Fran's pauses.

"Thanks Fran. So, what did I miss yesterday?"

"Only the biggest thing to happen to us in years!" Lester blurted, somewhat uncharacteristically. Justine could not immediately determine whether it was emotion, excitement, or just impatience that was behind his sudden interjection.

"It certainly would be very interesting," Fran added, "from what I have heard. Lots of people are talking about it."

Justine looked at Matt, pausing as if to invite him to speak. Matt carefully looked at Fran and Lester, then Justine, seeming quietly to be taking it all in.

"So just exactly what is this big news?" Justine asked the group, not sure who would respond.

"The big news," replied Lester, almost before Justine had gotten all the words in her question out, "is that SciTech International is interested in our product." His tone was terse, even a bit hostile, Justine felt, and she wondered if Lester held her somehow at fault for not being in the office the day before to hear the news herself.

"SciTech would be our biggest client by far," Lester continued. "They have very specific requirements."

"They have also apparently done a lot of value-chain analysis recently," added Fran, "and have interest in potentially centralizing their supplier relationships. Which means, if we work well with them, there could be other opportunities for expanding the relationship."

"Like product innovation." That was Lester, blurting again. "But we have got to get moving on this. Nick's team is already off and running!"

The room brimmed with enthusiasm and energy, but Justine also sensed some uncertainty. She could see the team looking to her for direction. It was if she held an imaginary starter gun and they were waiting to hear the sound of the shot. But Justine decided to stick with her planned agenda.

"Well, it seems that is news indeed," she started, sensing Lester was already growing impatient with her, "and we'll get back to it. But for now, let's stay on task. Matt, how have you been coming along with the review of our control procedures?"

Matt cleared his throat. "I am roughly 75% complete with the review, and have listed in this file the exceptions noted to date," he said as he handed out a two-page document. "I will continue to keep this current as I complete the analysis. This is available on the LAN if anyone wants a softcopy of it."

As Justine completed her agenda items, Lester's shoulders sunk and he peered out the open door. Fran tapped a pencil on the table and looked distracted. The meeting was quickly completed. Justine thanked the team for their time and let them know she would investigate the SciTech situation and get back to them shortly. Each lead departed quickly, walking silently back to their desks.

Justine could not help but think that her meeting could have gone better. In fact, the further back towards her office she walked the more convinced she was that she should have done something different and better. She was unhappy that the meeting seemed to end on a weak note, as well as having left the big issue open on the table. But beyond that, she continued to weigh her reactions to the coaching session from the day before. She wondered whether she should pursue her instinct to change the way she did business at SPI, or move in the opposite direction—and assuming she could decide which way to go, she wondered how fast she should move.

CHAPTER FOUR

OFF AND RUNNING

As she turned to head into her office, Justine realized that in her preoccupied thinking before the meeting she had not gotten any coffee for herself. Justine never drank coffee in college, but nowadays each morning usually started with hot cup.

Back in her office, Justine checked messages. The first was from Nick, left shortly after seven that morning, regarding the SciTech news. Funny, Justine thought, that Nick hadn't mentioned SciTech when she ran into him in the kitchenette.

Justine thought about the big news. SciTech International was one of the top companies in the world. They regularly posted impressive revenues and net income, and by virtually all other measures seemed always on a trajectory toward enviable performance. Known worldwide as one of the leading innovators in business, they were also frequently praised for a corporate culture built around transparency and openness.

Certainly it was no wonder that her team was at once both enthused and antsy by the SciTech prospect. Lester's comment about Nick's team—that they were "off and running"—bothered Justine. SciTech's headquarters was in her territory. It would certainly be a challenge for Justine to pull her team together to address SciTech's daunting requirements. But still, why was Nick involved?

Scanning her calendar, Justine was reminded that she had a one-on-one meeting with her boss the next afternoon. She thought about going in to see him immediately. Clearly, she had not been as "in the loop" on the SciTech news as Nick was, and somebody else told her team in her absence. Maybe her boss could shed some light on that. Justine stopped herself, though. She knew she was naturally impatient to resolve issues. Would interrupting her boss be seen critically or unfavorably?

Justine's calendar showed a few open hours early that afternoon. She decided to use that time to walk around and see for herself how the floor was engaged, if at all, in the SciTech news. She would not bother her boss, yet.

The binder from yesterday's seminar still sat on her desk. Ironic, she thought, that at the same time she was soaking up diverse thinking that could help her move ahead in her new role as manager, she seemed to be losing ground back at the office.

Justine remembered that Meg Santiago, one of the speakers at the conference, talked about the need to actively train teams to think innovatively. The motivation for innovation training, Santiago observed, often comes from the top down, when senior management feels that the current quality of solutions or ideas is inadequate. She also said that similar drive can come from teams, when individuals determine that not enough is being done to find new and original solutions to challenges.

Turning to the tab for Santiago's session in the binder, Justine saw the familiar "dot" exercise and read the following:

Outside the Box
9-Dot Puzzle/Solution

In-the-box thinkers find it difficult to recognize the quality of an idea. An idea is an idea. A solution is a solution. In fact, these kinds of thinkers can be quite stubborn when it comes to valuing an idea. They rarely invest the time to turn a mediocre solution into a potentially great solution.

More importantly, in-the-box thinkers are skillful at killing ideas. They are masters of creativity-busting attitudes, such as "...that'll never work" or "...it's too risky." The best in-the-box thinkers may be truly unaware that they drain the enthusiasm and passion of innovative thinkers while they derail their innovative ideas.

They also believe that every problem needs only one solution; therefore, finding more than one possible solution is usually a waste of time. They often say, "There is no time for discussions or creative solutions. We just need THE solution."

Thinking outside the box requires different attributes that include:
• Willingness to take new perspectives on day-to-day work.
• Openness to both do different things and to do things differently.
• Focusing on the value of finding new ideas and acting upon them.
• Striving to create value in new ways.
• Sincerely listening to others.
• Supporting and respecting others when they come up with new ideas.

Out-of-the box thinking requires an openness to new ways of seeing the world and a willingness to explore. Out-of-the box thinkers know that new ideas need nurturing and support. They also know that having an idea is good but acting on it is more important: Results and impact are what count.

Justine recalled something her husband had read in a sports book by a famous coach. He would often repeat it to her: "At some point in everyone's life they need to plant their feet and make a stand about who they are and what they believe in." Justine had a hunch that for her, that time might be approaching fast.

CHAPTER FIVE

PARADE WALK

After lunch, Justine set off for what her father, a long-time military reservist, would have called a "parade walk." The business world had adopted the same principle under the moniker Management By Walking Around. She decided to first visit her team, and then work over to Nick's area, where she hoped to catch him in person.

She saw Fran at her desk as she approached her team's work area. Fran was looking at her computer when Justine arrived. She stopped and looked directly at her boss.

"Hi, Justine," Fran said, swiveling away from her monitor. "Have a seat?" She motioned toward her desk-side chair.

Since being promoted, Justine tried to divide her face-to-face time with her direct reports evenly. Sitting with one of her leads at their desk, she wondered if that person's colleagues would notice, and what other leads might think if she did not visit with them as well. This time Justine chose to ignore those pangs of concern and sat right down with Fran

"Thanks, Fran," Justine said as she sat down. "Do you have a few minutes?"

"Sure, Justine," Fran said with a smile. "What can I do for you?"

"Well, maybe you can clue me in to what happened yesterday. It seems I picked a lousy day to be away."

"You shouldn't take Lester too seriously," Fran said. "He thinks he has the whole deal figured out. And he's already working on product specs and change orders."

"Really?" Justine was utterly curious as to why most people felt so at ease talking one way while in a meeting or more public setting, and such a different way in private or one-on-one.

"Anyway," Fran continued in the same tone, "the news broke late yesterday morning. Les and his tech pals got wind of it first. I actually heard about it from Matt. By that time, word was spreading quickly. The first thing I did, of course, was jump on the computer to start researching SciTech."

"Matt, hmm," Justine said, nodding her head. "Interesting."

"From what I understand," Fran said, "SciTech is looking for a new global partner. This deal could be twice the size of any we have now with existing customers. But they want certain innovations written into the contract. Stuff we aren't sure if we can do. It's in our territory so it's our deal, right Justine? Even if it is SciTech. This could be huge for all of us."

"Thanks, Fran," Justine said. "I appreciate your time. For now, just keep up with work in progress. We'll chat about SciTech shortly." With that Justine rose from Fran's chair, smiled and stepped out of Fran's desk area.

"Sure thing," Fran said. "But please keep me in the loop, OK? I always feel like I'm the last to know. Thanks."

"Will do," Justine replied, sensing her sincerity. Justine nodded her head and smiled again—trying to look reassuring, not knowing if Fran recognized that Justine, in fact, was the last to know about SciTech.

Past the LAN station, Justine headed over to Matt's cubicle. Matt had two binders and a spiral-bound packet open at his desk, and seemed intently engaged in work. He didn't notice Justine until she tapped gently on the side of his cubicle.

"Hi, Justine," Matt responded, wheeling away from his desk a bit. "How are you?"

"Good, Matt. Thanks." Justine replied. "How are you?"

"Fine, thanks. I'm looking over these various specs from the past few design modifications—lots of interesting possibilities." Justine wasn't sure how to read Matt's fidgety body language. Was he timid, she wondered, intimidated, or something else altogether.

"Well, that's good," Justine said. "SciTech is going to take all the possibilities we can dream up. By the way, I'm sorry I missed all the excitement yesterday. How did you first hear about the whole SciTech deal?"

"From Les at first," Matt said. "I mentioned it to Fran, but it seemed by then everybody knew."

"Just so I'm clear, Matt, who do you mean by everybody?" Justine asked. She tried conscientiously to keep her tone calm even though she felt herself begin to doubt the whole line of inquiry.

"Nick's team, really." Matt replied. "Nora and Sean seemed pretty pumped-up about the whole thing."

Feeling her cheeks flush, Justine began to think she should have visited Nick first. Why would Nick's team be working on a prospect in her territory? And why would Nick not come right out and say so? Especially if he knew something about it yesterday

"Thanks, Matt," Justine said. "And thanks for helping to keep our team in the loop. I know Fran appreciates it and so do I. Let me chat with Nick and I'll get back to you."

"No problem," Matt replied.

Justine stood up, gave Matt a smile and a nodding, positive look of appreciation. Next stop was Lester's desk, which turned out to be a beehive of activity. Rapidly scribbled poster-size schemas were strewn around the cubicle. Lester was deep in conversation with three colleagues, one of whom was making notes on a mobile whiteboard.

She could see that they were discussing product specs and it looked like SciTech requirements from what she could make out on the board. She stopped, thinking specifically about whether to attempt to interrupt him. Justine could almost feel the umbrage Lester might come back with if she disturbed them in the middle of their working session. Thinking she was perhaps taking the easy way out, she decided not to intrude on Lester at that point. She decided to talk with Nick first and then circle back with Lester.

Nick, Justine concluded, should help put a few more needed pieces together if she and her team were going to function in any proper capacity to respond to the new prospect. She was confident in her leads, and pleased that they were taking initiative.

She knew her team could be successful. What she didn't know was that her visit with Nick would set in motion a series of events which would significantly impact SPI and its budding deal with SciTech, as well as propel one of them forward in their careers. A visit which would also indirectly deliver Justine to the brink of her ambitions, even though she was not yet fully aware of what they were.

CHAPTER SIX

HEARING AND LISTENING

Laughing could be heard from Nick's office as Justine turned the corner and approached his open door. Sitting in front of his desk were Nick's leads, Nora Johnson and Sean Lassiter.

Both Nora and Sean had worked with Nick at his previous employer, an SPI competitor. Nora was the more technical of the two, while Sean was a strong project manager. They seemed to work well as a team and exhibited a sense of pride in their work. Nick's group had a consistent track record at SPI of solid performance—in contrast, Justine couldn't help but think, with her own team's peaks and valleys.

Nick and his team also appeared to have a rapport with one another. Justine had always attributed it to the fact that they had worked together for a long period of time. They cultivated a kind of "in crowd" culture, eating lunch together regularly, socializing after hours, and going out of their way to help each other. While Justine surely admired that, she couldn't think of a time when they actually went out of their way to help another team, hers or anyone else's.

Slowing as she approached his doorway, Justine turned into Nick's office. The laughter stopped. In what felt like a split second, a certain discomfort somehow overtook the fresh silence in the room.

"Nick, do you have a couple minutes?" Justine asked. She was instantly unsure whether the words came out sounding strange. She was all of the sudden a bit nervous.

"You bet, Justine. We were just about done anyway," Nick responded, composedly. "Hey, guys, thanks. Give us a few minutes and we'll catch up later."

Nora and Sean, quietly watching since Justine's arrival, glided silently out the door, pausing only to exchange a quick glance with Nick.

"O.K., Justine," Nick continued after his leads had departed, "what's on your mind?"

"Well, I wanted to talk with you about this SciTech prospect. I heard about it this morning from my team and it seems to be..."

"The SciTech deal is huge, Justine," Nick interrupted. "This could get SPI to the next level. They are the kind of player we have been waiting for."

There was a brief pause. Justine had so many questions running through her head. She wasn't sure where to go first.

"Who's the 'we,' Nick?"

"I'm not sure what you mean."

"Who's the 'we' you said have been waiting for this kind of deal," Justine repeated. She wondered if her voice gave away the fact that she was nervous.

"Well, SPI of course. And my team."

Justine felt both frustration and confusion rising at the same time. An image came to her mind of Nick as a star quarterback, the kind who liked to call the signals and had a practiced smile for the cameras. The kind who sometimes remembered to thank his teammates, but always made sure the spotlight stayed on him.

Justine pictured herself in a different mold, perhaps that of a coach on the sidelines or in the booth. Not as the star. Justine wanted her team and her leads to share the spotlight.

Nick leaned back in his chair.

"SciTech is actually in our territory," Justine stated. She knew Nick would know which 'our' she meant.

"Justine, no offense," Nick quickly answered back, "but this deal requires deep knowledge, experience, and adaptability. My team has been at this business for a while, and I personally want to help make sure this is successful. These deals don't come along everyday, you know."

"I'm not sure what you mean, Nick. Are you saying my team somehow isn't qualified?" Justine asked. "Why shouldn't they be the ones driving the project? And if this is our biggest customer ever, maybe we should all be working together on it."

Nick sat square in his chair and stood up, as if ready to show his guest to the door. "Justine, that's a great idea," he said tersely. "Sit tight and I'm sure there's a role for everyone. There's plenty of room at the table."

Justine took the hint that their conversation was coming to a close, at least for now. But it was clear that they were not on the same page. "Nick, I am not sure this conversation is finished," she told him, sensing the conflict inherent in the comment.

Nick took a breath and looked out the door. "Look, Justine, I'm sure this is important to you…"

Not the way you think it is, she thought.

"…but I'm sure senior management wants our most tenured team here." They stepped into the hallway. "And like you said yesterday, you're still a new manager!"

Justine debated about whether to try to score a point against Nick or to be more diplomatic.

"I appreciate your time, Nick," Justine said, "and like I said before, I think this conversation will need to continue. Thanks."

With that she gave Nick a look in the eye, a flat smile, and turned to walk down the corridor back to her office. She knew Nick was delighted to have the discussion over with, and could almost feel the tension level lessen with every step she took away from his office. She couldn't help but replay pieces of the dialogue in her head and question what she said and did, what she didn't say, how stilted her thinking and the whole dynamic became. She was privately pleased with how she closed the discourse, but was not sure what, if anything was actually accomplished.

CHAPTER SEVEN

CHALLENGING COMPLACENCY

For the rest of the day, Justine threw herself into busywork to keep her mind off the immediate challenges she faced. By the time she finished responding to emails and voicemails, SPI's offices were mostly dark.

She knew that her team was looking to her for direction. As she reran the conversation with Nick in her head, she continued to think of other, better questions, and better replies. Despite Nick's comments, Justine was confident in her team's ability to deliver. She was concerned, though, about what Nick might say to others about her team. Frustrated, Justine looked for another distraction.

The diversity binder was still on her desk, pushed to the side under a few folders. Justine thought back to Victor Jamison's session and the seminar's final hour. Were there other possibilities out there? She found her notes about the qualities that define coaching, and studied the bulleted list the group had developed. Were there clues in the list for resolving her situation?

She had stapled Victor Jamison's business card to her notes. She looked at the clock. She looked at the business card. What would people say if she called a professional, executive coach? What would her peers think? Her leads? What would her boss think? What would her husband Fred think?

Fred would probably understand. Fred was a big sports fan, and followed coaches as much as players. He would frequently talk about the likes of John Wooden, Tom Landry, Joe Gibbs, and Scotty Bowman. They were successful with different teams, different players, in different eras, and in some cases even different sports. Innovators even as they carried on great traditions, they often authored their own playbooks, having learned themselves from great mentors, and always surrounded themselves with a talented, trusted staff of experts, not a bunch of yes-men. They were the type of leaders who would never accept complacency, or fold in the face of adversity.

Regarding SciTech, Justine knew that she needed to act. But intuition told her that she needed better perspective on the situation. She did have important concerns about her team's ability to work together, and their ability to work with Nick, his team, and senior management. She realized she also had some doubts about her ability to lead her team, especially given the tension around the project and the high stakes that SciTech represented as SPI's most significant prospect ever.

Of one thing Justine was absolutely certain: she was not about to give up. She was determined that her team would succeed, and she was not going to let the questions, uncertainties, or obstacles derail them. She had also started to realize after the day's events that she was frankly less concerned with SciTech per se, and really more concerned about her team and her ability to lead them.

Justine knew she had a one-on-one with her boss the next afternoon—and a mess to sort out. Not sure if she was working inside or outside the box, she promptly called the telephone number on Victor Jamison's business card.

CHAPTER EIGHT

KINGS AND QUEENS

Guy McNamara was SPI's president and CEO. A twenty-year veteran with an Ivy League MBA, Guy had quickly worked through the ranks and numerous rotations. He was appointed president early in his tenure, then added the CEO title a few years later. Despite his meteoric rise to senior management, Guy worked hard to stay connected with frontline SPI employees and customers.

Guy would schedule periodic breakfasts and lunches with employees. This was a fairly typical practice for a CEO, but Guy took the sessions extremely seriously. He would come with a list of questions, take notes, entertain questions from the group, and always follow-up. Guy personally tried to make every one of these sessions better than the last.

He knew how important his personal visits were. He paid special attention to interactions like handshakes, eye contact, and tone of voice. He had met Justine at one of the lunches he sponsored, and was impressed by her preparation, candor, and demeanor.

Justine reported to Harvey Mumford, who was also Nick's boss. A vice president, Harvey reported directly to Guy McNamara. With SPI for more than 30 years, Harvey had spent his tenure in basically the same role. His focus was predominantly on bottom-line results. As the company grew, Harvey was a frequent critic of ever-expanding employee development programs. Harvey often said that recent hires at SPI had a far easier time than he and his colleagues had endured during the company's difficult early days.

Justine began reporting to Harvey when she was promoted. They met one-on-one in regularly scheduled monthly meetings. Justine generally prepared a discussion document, which she emailed to Harvey the day before their meeting. She also brought two copies to the meeting, since Harvey never had one printed out (and, she sensed, probably never looked at it in advance).

This time, though, Justine decided not to send her boss any discussion document in advance. She had scheduled a meeting with Victor Jamison right before her one-on-one with Harvey, and she couldn't be sure how, or if, that conversation might change her intentions for the meeting with her boss.

At 11:55 the next morning, Justine was back in the lobby of the Crown Plaza hotel, waiting for Victor Jamison. The hotel was convenient and had plenty of good places to sit and talk. Justine appreciated that it was also the place where she had first been struck by what Victor had to say about coaching.

Minutes later, Justine was watching the revolving door as Victor slowly turned through. She was standing alone off to the opposite side of the front desk, and Victor walked directly to her and held out his hand.

"Good afternoon. I am Victor Jamison. You are Justine Fullerton, I presume."

"Yes, I'm Justine. Thanks for agreeing to meet with me."

They found a couple of comfortable chairs in a nook off the main lobby. Justine was struck by Victor's calm demeanor as he placed his coat over the arm of the chair and patiently pulled a notebook out of his briefcase. He folded his hands on the table and looked pleasantly, calmly at Justine. Victor started their conversation.

"Well, Justine, I am delighted to make your acquaintance. How can I assist you?"

Justine had been trying to plan what to say and how to say it since they had scheduled the meeting the night before. She brought him up to speed about her situation at work. She also talked about her reaction to his session on coaching, and how his messages resonated with her. She ended with uncertain questions about what coaching really was, whether even calling him was a good idea, and how much it might cost, but added that her husband, Fred, was supportive.

Victor smiled and looked encouragingly at Justine. "Let me start by saying that coaching is focused on learning and developing potential. A coach listens to feelings as well as facts, for clues as to how to get the client to the next action step. A coach can also help clients clarify their own values, and align their actions to them."

Justine nodded.

"If you are interested, and with your permission," Victor continued, "I am happy to discuss with you your work situation as your executive coach."

Victor and Justine talked for the rest of the hour. She took several pages of notes. She emphasized two key items with thick underscores.

1) Relative to my impending one-on-one with Harvey:
Executives are like royalty—some are benevolent dictators,
some are servant leaders, and others are autocratic rulers.
Do I know who at SPI is which type, and how to deal with
them accordingly, have meaningful conversations with them?
2) There are three kinds of conversations:
  · Conversations for Understanding
  · Conversations for Possibilities
  · Conversations for Action

Reflecting on her recent meetings at SPI, Justine told Victor, "I think I have been trying to have conversations for understanding, while everybody else was in a conversation for action. Well, on second thought maybe Fran and Matt were trying to have a conversation for possibilities. I'm sure I am not the only one frustrated, but I know I am the one who needs to do something about it."

At the end of their meeting, Justine and Victor agreed to meet again the following week. Justine headed back to the office with renewed energy and eagerness. She had a strong feeling that she was moving in the right direction, and picking up momentum.

PART TWO

ON THE RUNWAY

There are risks and costs to a program of action. But they are far less than the long-range risks and costs of comfortable inaction.

—John F. Kennedy

I believe that one of life's greatest risks is never daring to risk.

—Oprah Winfrey

CHAPTER NINE

HELP IS NOT ON THE WAY

The next week, Justine hurried to the Crown Plaza to again meet with Victor. She looked panoramically around the lobby, and then focused on the table nestled off to the side of the entryway where she and Victor had met last week.

He was waiting for her this time, looking relaxed, his jacket again hung neatly over the arm of his chair. Justine smiled and sat down in the seat opposite Victor, laying her notepad on the tabletop.

"Thanks for meeting me again," Justine began. "I have been thinking a lot about our last discussion and wanted to ask a few questions, and maybe share with you what happened."

"Sounds great," Victor replied. "Where would you like to start?"

"Well, first off, at a high level could you go over the conversation process again? I was trying to explain it to my husband."

"Sure. Let's remember that listening and speaking both occur in the context of conversations," Victor began. "The basic unit of human interaction is conversation: people relate with each other and get things done through conversations. This was one of the primal communication technologies, believe it or not!"

"Right, and even emails and phone calls are kinds of conversations," Justine added.

"Absolutely," continued Victor. "And different types of conversations generate different outcomes. The more capable you are in distinguishing different types of conversations, and how to utilize them in different circumstances, the better you can shape those outcomes."

"Like the one-on-one with Harvey, my boss, which I had after we met last time," Justine replied.

"Right," Victor said. "And there are three types of conversations. Only three." He held up three fingers and affably raised his eyebrows. "Conversations for understanding, conversations for possibilities, and conversations for action."

Victor asked Justine to list the communications and conversations in which she regularly engaged at work and the venues where they took place. As she listed them under two headings, Victor wrote "Communication" on top and "Conversations" on the bottom, linking them with a big circle:

Communication

Connections	*Venues*
-Person to Person	New-hire training -
- Person to group/sub team	Manager 1-1s -
-Person to team	Peer 1-1s -
-Person to department	Mentoring -
-Person to organization	Coaching -
-Organization to person	Formal training -
-Department to person	On-the-job training -
-Team to person	Broadcast messages -
-Group/sub team to person	Town-halls -
-Another person to person	Staff meetings -
-Person to him/herself	Performance management -

Conversations

"Organizations are networks of conversations, really," Victor said. "So much of how work gets done is accomplished through ordinary conversations."

"Some days it seems like a lot of talking and not much forward progress," Justine affirmed. Victor nodded.

"Within all these communications there are three types of conversations happening: for *understanding*, for *possibilities*, and for *action*," he said. "How well we perform in many ways is predicated on our ability to be successful in those conversations."

"What do you mean?" asked Justine, pulling her chair in a bit further.

"Let's take a typical scenario," Victor replied. "Say you're managing a call center and volumes are running so high your customer service is in jeopardy. You would get a team of people in a room to address the situation, right?"

"Sounds right so far." Justine had stopped taking notes and was carefully listening to the example.

"Well, in that meeting room, the conversation would ordinarily start with some kind of understanding: why are we here, who is represented in the room, what circumstance brought us together—in this case, the high volumes—and that what is needed is some sort of remedy."

"What typically happens then," Victor continued, "is that the group engages in a discussion of potential remedies, or 'possibilities.' This usually goes on for as long as folks can stand. It's usually not long before someone says 'we need a solution!' Then the conversation switches suddenly from discussing possibilities to talking about taking action."

"Generally, as soon as the action discussion begins, all 'possibility' talk ends," Victor said. "Then, assignments are made and sometimes noted. Typically within 45 minutes or so from starting the meeting, a course of action has been selected and assigned and the meeting adjourns."

"Understanding, possibilities, action—I can see the meeting moved through those types or phases," Justine said. "I would think that most meetings or conversations flow through them. Wouldn't they?"

"Yes," Victor replied. "Individuals who can distinguish between the types of conversations may be able to determine if the phasing or shifting from one type to another is useful or counterproductive. How many of those people in the meeting do you think fully understood the situation, or had properly exhausted the reasonable possibilities—perhaps simply recycling old ideas—and were fully prepared and committed to clear, coordinated action with sufficient conditions of satisfaction?"

Justine looked puzzled.

"There are certainly times when conversations work extremely well," Victor said. "The call center meeting is an example, of course, of a poor conversation. In meetings like that, teams of management regularly short-cut genuine understanding by all parties, or simply exhibit limited listening, which narrows participation and diverse thinking. That stifles innovation and creativity by squeezing possibilities. And then the group succumbs to impatience with regard to action steps."

"That sounds like my meeting with Nick, and my weekly team meeting," Justine said. "I was trying to understand the situation while others were bent on taking action. We couldn't get on the same page. We wasted time, raised everybody's frustration levels, and put the real solution that much further out."

Victor nodded.

Justine smiled and looked amusingly at her coach. "Rather than being at the end of figuring this out," she said, "I am starting to realize I am just at the beginning."

"Others certainly cannot do it for you," Victor said. "And it may get more challenging before it improves. Keep in mind that you are in a different place now than you were just one week ago. You now more clearly perceive your own conversations. You have begun to broaden and build your capability to observe, but also your way of being in those conversations—*understanding, possibilities,* and *action*—which will unlock tremendous performance and effectiveness previously hidden."

Justine and Victor closed their conversation by scheduling a series of future weekly meetings at the Crown Plaza.

CHAPTER TEN

GREENER GRASS

At SPI, the SciTech prospect was being actively developed. Harvey, Justine and Nick's boss, had not made a clear decision on who "owned" the relationship so Justine, Nick, and their teams, continued to try to work on it together. The process was anything but smooth, as the teams debated approaches to winning the deal.

That week, Justine and Victor met at the Crown Plaza as planned.

"How's it going?" Victor asked, settling into his usual chair.

"Well, let's just say we haven't hit our stride yet," Justine replied. "I think I am engaging in conversations more purposefully, understanding the types, but I'm not sure the results are there."

"O.K.," Victor said. "We know language consists of listening and speaking, and that conversations are fundamental in creating our perceptions of reality." He paused a moment, to let Justine reflect for a moment on his last phase.

"Language is the fundamental human technology," Victor continued. "Conversations and language are used to produce outcomes and generate perceptions of reality. People act or behave based on their own perception of reality. Effective leadership, management, team behavior, and even coaching depend heavily on how people use language. What is done, and how well it is done, is shaped by how people do and do not use language."

"We all react to what we see and hear," Justine said, picking up on what Victor was saying. "I experience this all the time. If we think someone is against our position, we close up. If we hear and feel support and openness, more ideas and enthusiasm flow."

"I am glad you mentioned that, Justine," Victor said. "Listening, or hearing, is critical. Much more so than managers typically recognize."

"What do you mean?" Justine asked, tightening her grip on her pen in preparation to write.

"Listening is an ever-present part of human interaction in the workplace," Victor responded. "Listening is the crucial factor in communication, and essential for establishing trust and rapport. Listening is really a core business process."

"Research has recently shown that managers, much like you," Victor opened his hand towards Justine as he spoke, "spend much of their time engaged in listening. Does the listening of these managers facilitate new ideas and positive change, as well as enhance performance and effectiveness?"

"I would say generally not," Justine answered. "We are typically so rushed and think more about the immediate outcome of the problem or issue at hand than we do about the conversation intended to address that issue."

"Well said," Victor offered. Justine smiled and turned to a new page in her notebook. "Speaking of which, speaking itself is certainly another key business process," Victor continued. "And there are six precise linguistic tools—also called basic linguistic acts, or speech acts—that humans use in everyday conversations to create reality and get things done. Most people are not aware of how they use, or misuse, these linguistic tools. Awareness of how to intentionally use them produces more effective ways of conversing, relating, and performing, in the workplace and elsewhere."

"Six?" Justine asked. "There are six for all humans?"

"There are six," Victor confirmed. "They are: 1) Assessments, 2) Assertions, 3) Declarations, 4) Requests, 5) Offers, and 6) Promises."

Victor pulled a laminated 5x7 card from his briefcase and placed it on the table in between him and Justine. "These six represent language at work, home, even in our own heads—our private conversations."

He reviewed each speech act one at a time, along with their examples and definitions:

Speech Act	Example	Definition
Assessment	• We are making progress. • The client loves us. • Every time this happens for the same reasons.	A statement of opinion. May or may not be based on grounded information.
Assertion	• All tasks were completed on schedule. • It's raining outside • This is our largest prospect ever	Statement of fact. Empirical evidence is generally available.
Declaration	• I will be on time from now on. • We will not lose this account. • We will put a man on the moon and safely return him to the earth.	Making a statement to shape future actions. Creating a space of action publicly or privately.
Request	• Could you have this by noon? • Please review and provide feedback?	Asking for a statement of commitment. Often with specific conditions of satisfaction included.
Offer	• Would you like me to send it? • I can schedule the meeting, if you like?	Offering something specific. Usually by a specific time or with certain conditions of satisfaction.
Promise	• It will be on your desk by 5 p.m. • You will have our completed response by our next meeting.	Statement of commitment. Provides something particular by a specific time or with certain conditions of satisfaction.

"These speech acts make up the language we use, hear, and think of as we engage in conversations throughout our lives."

"I'm sorry, but I'm not sure I 'get it' yet," Justine admitted.

"For example," Victor said, "my daughter *requests* permission to go to a movie, *asserts* that the movie is playing at a specific theater, and *promises* to come back home by a specific time. I *offer* to pick her up and she *declares* her gratitude with a thank-you.

"Here's another," Victor continued. "A customer or client *asks* for a product. You *assert* that you have it in stock and *offer* to deliver it at a specific time at his or her office. When he or she receives it, the customer *declares* satisfaction with the product (or *declares* his or her dissatisfaction if the product fails to meet expectations)."

"I think I understand," Justine said, reviewing the notes she had just taken.

"Let's try looking at it this way," Victor replied. "How much of the time in meetings are you clear what is an assessment versus what is an assertion—knowing fact from opinion?"

"Maybe half, the rest of the time I'm not sure."

"And what are the implications if one is unsure? What happens when an assessment is taken as an assertion? Suppose Lester blurts out to the team, 'we're behind, we've got to catch up?' Is that an assessment or an assertion?"

"Hmm, sounds like an assessment, his opinion."

"And what impact does that have on others in the conversation?"

"Well, they would see that Lester is the most tenured person on the team and would likely take his opinion as being factual—meaning they would act in accordance with his assessment."

Victor paused. "At what risk?" Victor asked Justine.

"At the risk of rushing to a course of action prematurely, for one," she replied, "and perhaps wrongly pitting competition against collaboration. I am not sure anyone is actually ahead or behind, just at different stages of development."

"Taking assessment as assertions can be incredibly damaging," Victor said. "It can not only limit future potential, but can hamper current daily efforts. Add to this the impact of unclear promises, vague conditions of satisfactions…"

"…And it feels like an average status meeting where there is lots of talking and not much forward progress," Justine said. "Certainly not as much collaborative focus on the key things needed."

"Absolutely," Victor said. "Viewing language as speech acts opens up an important field of learning. If we improve our ability to communicate, we can substantially increase our effectiveness, our coordination of actions with others, our personal well-being, and our personal power."

"It becomes easier to recognize the power of observation," he continued, "and the ability to act more powerfully when we are able to 'view' our conversations and coordinate action based on our understanding of the speech acts involved. Improving these fundamental components of communication can solve many of the conflicts and problems we face in our personal and organizational lives."

"Now let me try a few examples," Justine said. "An employee who can overcome his or her discomfort or difficulty in saying 'no' to requests can stop from feeling overwhelmed. Their frustration may be due to the absence of a request for help. They could be ineffective due to an inability to declare their lack of knowledge in important areas—what I call knowing what we don't know. A lack of innovation may be due to the absence of speculative conversations. And resignation or lack of motivation may be caused by the absence of a declaration that allows us to become motivated and aligned with a particular mission!"

"I think you've got it!" Victor said, smiling.

Smiling back, Justine said, "Well, I'm getting it, little by little."

CHAPTER ELEVEN

DON'T FIX WHAT'S NOT BROKEN

At her next meeting with Victor, Justine was noticeably tense.

"Well, I think I may have made a wrong move," she told him. "I get the sense that I may, to be very honest, be annoying people."

"What makes you think that? What did you observe?" Victor asked.

"O.K.," Justine started. "My speech acts are kind of amazing. I have been able to essentially translate language into speech acts during conversations at work and even at home. It helps really understand what people are saying. It's like all of the sudden I can hear with total clarity and my responses are unmistakably clear."

"That's wonderful! So where's the problem?" Victor asked.

"Not everyone else is 'translating,' and I think my excitement with it is negatively impacting others. They seem to be getting irritated. It seems the more I let my passion out the more annoyance I sense."

"People are always in some mood or emotion," Victor said. "Moods and emotions permeate everything people do. Recognizing, managing, and shifting moods and emotions is a crucial part of being a leader."

Justine nodded and started taking notes.

"The power of moods and emotions is that they always predispose people toward certain behaviors and away from others," Victor continued. "Speaking and listening, engaging in conversations—these are indispensable forms of interactions among people. They're our primal communication technology, if you will. How effectively people speak and listen cannot be separated from their moods and emotions, and from its impact on their behavior."

"Victor, I'm sorry if I am being dense here," Justine said. "I understand what you're saying, the words at least, but emotions and moods are invisible. And although it is the 21st century, we don't really talk about emotions at the workplace. I'm not sure I'm following you."

Victor smiled. "Unfortunately," he said, "moods and emotions have not been seen as a crucial area of learning for performance improvement. They are, however, an integral part of the successful use of language for effective communication in leadership, management, coaching, and team building. They form a central dimension of morale and employee performance."

Justine's look told Victor that she was still confused.

"Think of the last meeting you had, and how did you feel at the end of it?" Victor asked.

Justine thought for a moment. "I had a status meeting this morning with our entire department. At the end I felt flat, maybe a little disappointed that we weren't further along in the big deal with SciTech."

"Might you call that a mood of acknowledgement?"

"Sure. I was not enthused, but also not negative," Justine said.

"What drove you to that emotion? Why do you think that's where you ended up?" Victor asked. Justine sensed he already knew the answer.

"The tone of the meeting was not great," Justine responded. "Harvey, my boss, did most of the talking and he basically told us how behind schedule we were and that senior management was looking at us to perform. He focused pretty clearly on the bottom line."

"Was your assessment of the message more hopeful or disengaged?" Victor asked.

"Definitely disengaged," Justine replied. "Our teams left more deflated than when they arrived."

"How could the message have been different?" Victor asked. "What might Harvey, or you—either as a leader or member of the group—have done to create a more positive reaction, and more enthusiasm?"

"Well," Justine said, "for one thing focusing on the goal ahead and not the troubles in the past would be a start. Then encouraging future actions to inspire confidence and teamwork rather than reviewing complaints by management. And, importantly, I would not just modify the words themselves, but also the tone and excitement behind the message."

"And how might the results be different?" Victor asked.

"People work better when they are enthusiastic," Justine said. "People work together more when they feel that a hopeful, positive outcome is readily at hand."

"Exactly," Victor said. "There's no question that moods shape possibilities. Most of us have had the experience of working with an individual with a bad—or let's say ineffective-for-the-situation—mood or emotion. That individual's mood may be cynical or resigned. Similarly, the mood or emotion may be inappropriately positive, such as failing to see impending jeopardy or urgency. Whether positive or negative, moods are infectious. And when left unattended, the mood of a team will drift."

"I can certainly attest to that," Justine stated.

Victor nodded and continued, "Experiencing moods is both physiological, meaning oriented as a feeling in the body, and linguistic, an assessment disposed positively or negatively to the future. Moods often arise out of our past experiences. For example, a mood of anxiety may coincide with the recognition that we have struggled with a similar outcome in the past. And for a team that faces numerous possibilities, one member may see only limited or no possibilities, and her mood of resignation can infect the entire team."

"One way we gain access to moods is by investigating the conversations that constitute the mood, as in your example of the department meeting. Keep in mind though, that the conversation can be unarticulated, meaning part of a private thought."

"For example," Justine interjected, "A mood of resignation sounds like 'nothing is possible here. There is nothing I can do that will matter,' when the statement is untrue."

"Right," Victor said. "That individual is living in an assessment, and by characterizing the situation as one of no possibility, the individual shapes a space without possibilities. The action required is to reshape the assessment to one that is appropriate for the situation. The reshaping can start by examining the mood."

"O.K., so how do we do that?" Justine asked while taking notes.

"We start," Victor said, "by distinguishing moods and emotions. We recognize and utilize the basic moods of life as a deeper level of emotional intelligence, knowing how they impact morale and performance. We as leaders learn how to shift from negative moods to positive moods, and how to use moods and emotions to have more effective and influential conversations that build relationships and foster collaboration."

Justine scribbled notes feverishly.

"As human beings we go about our lives trying to make sense of things," Victor said. "We come up with explanations, and apply relevance and context in creating the 'story' of our own lives. Emotions and moods are as much a part of that story as are the words and pictures."

CHAPTER TWELVE

LEADING WITH YOUR CHIN

Waiting in the hotel lobby for his next meeting with Justine, Victor reflected on their past sessions. They had covered many important topics. What was not clear yet, though, was how much of what they had been discussing had converted into improved performance for Justine, her team, and, ultimately, SPI.

Justine arrived and asked Victor how he was doing.

"I have a bit of a cold, but I'm fine." Victor replied. "How are you doing?"

"Good, thanks." Justine sat back in the plush chair. "I think I have been more attuned to the emotional and moods dimension, and have continued to improve conversations through language."

"Glad to hear it," Victor said. "What are some of the improvements?"

"Well, in my team meeting, for the first time we all actually enjoyed some laughter. Fran had prepared a recognition of sorts for Matt's birthday (which I approved of, just a cake and a few guests from other departments he frequently works with), and as I looked around the room I saw that everyone, even Lester, was relaxed, sitting back in their chairs, laughing and enjoying themselves. It was really nice to see."

"That's great, and it's great you picked that up," Victor commented. "Our work life—and personal life as well—can be seen as an ongoing interplay between our language, our emotions, and our body. We have talked about language and emotions. We have not talked much about body or physical presence yet."

"Do you mean body language?" Justine asked.

"Yes," Victor said, "but it's more than just that. Who and how we are, at any particular point in time, is a dynamic and evolving interplay between language, emotions, and body. A prominent biologist once said that a constant 'braiding' of language and emotions occurs within people. Physiology and body posture is part of that 'braid' as well, if you will. Observing the body and intervening in how people are using their bodies or holding themselves physically is a key aspect in improving conversations."

"I can see a 'for example' coming," Justine said with a smile.

"Of course!" Victor said. "For example, consider the typical instance of a witness taking the stand in a courtroom. Jurors are certainly listening to what that witness has to say, but they are also observing the witness's body language, from the time that person's name is called to the moment they take the stand and throughout their testimony. The jurors watch how the witness walks, sits, and moves his or her body when they talk."

"I actually heard about something like that related to presidential debates," Justine said, "where viewers scored candidates with the sound on and off. The impact of their words was negligible compared to their physical presence."

"Exactly right, a great example," Victor said. "And again, this might seem a surprising area of attention with regard to performance improvement. Like moods and emotions though, the body has largely been ignored as a key area of learning that impacts individual and team performance."

"The body is always present in how people listen to each other and speak with each other," Victor continued. "Speaking is not limited to the sounds coming from our vocal chords. It occurs from the body as well. Just ask any stage actor or actress! In many delicate yet mighty ways, body posture can keep people trapped in negative moods, and negatively impact listening and speaking for them and others around them."

"That is so true. I've been a victim of it myself," Justine said. "So what about 'the how'? What can be done to address body posture?"

Victor coughed and took a deep breath before responding. "Specific techniques around the 'how' of addressing body posture include learning to use physical presence to get into more constructive and productive moods—individually and, importantly, with a team. Also, understanding how to leverage shifts in body posture, even small ones, can generate more positive interactions and produce more effective conversations."

"For example…" Justine said.

"A few examples," responded Victor. "Sitting upright when others are slouching to improve the mood, looking directly at people instead of around or away from them to get them engaged, getting up from a meeting and standing at a whiteboard or flipchart to focus attention, walking into a meeting room with a stride of confidence, lowering your voice and opening your hand toward an individual you want to pull into the conversation. More?"

"I think that's good," Justine replied, still writing notes. "I have a bunch more running through my head. It's incredible. These situations happen all the time, everyday. I can really see their usefulness and effectiveness."

"Good," said Victor. "Each of us has a unique way of being, which influences what we see and hear in the world around us. As you are realizing, we live predominantly in a world of interpretations, not facts, and our way of being determines how successfully we relate to both others and ourselves. And our way of being is based on a blend of our body, emotions, and language. Changes in any of those domains impact the other domains. For example, we influence our language and our bodies by altering our mood."

Justine sat up straight and grinned. "I declare my team is going to be doing a lot more laughing."

CHAPTER THIRTEEN

IT'S A SYSTEM, DUMMY

Justine ducked out of the rain into the Crown Plaza hotel. It was hard to believe another week had passed since she last met with Victor. She found her coach in their usual meeting place, a couple of comfortable chairs off the main lobby.

"So, how's it going this week?" Victor asked.

"The pressure's mounting. We are getting closer to the deadline for the SciTech proposal, but in terms of what needs to be done, we're only about halfway there," Justine replied. "I believe my team is working harder and more productively than ever, but there are just so many other factors and people involved."

"There always are," Victor commented. "We operate within a system larger than just ourselves and our teams, and our perceptions are just one piece of the whole."

"Is this like 'the team is more than the sum of its parts'?" asked Justine.

"In a way," responded Victor. "Though it's more that a feasible whole can be made from infeasible parts."

Justine began taking notes.

"Let me tell you a classic story from Persian literature," Victor began. "It's about a group of men who encounter a strange object in complete darkness. Since the storyteller is in the dark himself, he cannot provide any clues about the object. Each of the 'blind' men, positioned at different parts of the object, reports his finding from his respective position: 'it's a snake'; 'no, it's a pillar'; 'no, it's a fan'; 'no, it's a spear!' All efforts to identify the object by touching its different parts proved fruitless and frustrating until someone arrived with a light. Any guess what the object was?"

"I can't imagine," Justine replied, engrossed in the anecdote.

"The light enabled them all to see the whole at last: an elephant!" Victor said. "The story means that the ability to see the whole somehow requires an enabling light of some kind, one that would help advance our initial assumptions until a satisfactory vision of the whole is achieved."

"Sounds kind of like looking at the completed picture of a model airplane before starting to build it," Justine said.

"Yes, exactly right. Now consider trying to make sense of that same story, but with prior knowledge of the elephant."

"What do you mean?" asked Justine.

"Let me put it this way," Victor said. "If you were told that story again, you would likely experience no trouble in sorting out the distorted information and putting it in perspective, because you already know that the subject is an elephant. Right?"

"That's certainly true."

"And at that point, while we may sympathize with the men in the dark, we won't struggle along with them," Victor said. "It seems we need a preconceived notion of the whole before we can make sense of our respective position or role. Or, in other words, glean order out of chaos."

"Like the picture of the finished model plane," Justine said.

"If the entire team working on the proposal had the exact same conception of the whole, the same finished model plane," Victor said, "what would the implication be?"

"If we had a clear picture of a finished product, we could all 'divide and conquer.' We could each take a piece and build it, then bring it all together," Justine replied.

Victor paused briefly, gaining slightly more of Justine's attention as he caught her eye. "True. But only if everyone contributing has the exact same, clear picture of the finished product."

"Ah-ha," Justine commented. "Now I see what you mean. That actually explains a lot."

"Projects require people and teams to work together to produce results," Victor went on. "Each individual naturally brings something different to the project. And not just skills and competencies, but different past and present experiences, and differing capacities for learning, cooperating, improvising, sharing, and of course much more. Everyday coordination of action can be done 'blindly,' or with an enabling light."

CHAPTER FOURTEEN

BREAKDOWN

I think we are in a crisis," Justine reported, rushing to get settled at her next weekly coaching visit with Victor.

"What kind of crisis?" Victor asked.

"The SciTech proposal is in trouble," Justine explained. "It seems that while I thought my team and Nick's team were working together, at least a little bit, it turns out that his team has come up with an entire approach on their own and they plan to review it with senior management tomorrow."

"Really? Are you surprised?" Victor asked.

"Well, my team is pretty upset," Justine replied. "I am very disappointed, if not alarmed. I can't say I am actually surprised or shocked."

"It looks like you'll be stepping into a defining moment in short order," Victor said.

"What do you mean?"

"A Harvard professor once wrote that thoughtful managers will sooner or later face a business problem which raises difficult, often deeply personal questions," Victor answered. "A situation when managers must choose between right and right when deciding what to do."

"I think you might be right," Justine confirmed.

"Truly great leaders are also great coaches," Victor continued. "In my work with organizations and their executives, I have found that the most effective leaders consistently demonstrate several traits. There are seven traits." Victor held up seven fingers and smiled.

"Seven exactly?" Justine shot back, smirking.

"As you prepare for tomorrow, and continue your own learning in pursuit of leadership mastery, you may find that these are useful." Victor pulled a laminated card from his briefcase. He reviewed each of the seven traits with Justine, linking them to examples from their prior coaching conversations.

	Leadership Trait: The ability to...	Description
1	Forge conversations which encourage questioning existing presuppositions and perceptions.	Given that most actions come from a set of presuppositions, perceptions or assumptions from which individuals and teams operate, it is important to be able to identify them and effectively challenge them as appropriate.
2	Listen for ways of being (language, emotions/moods and physical presence).	The ability to discern what is true, right, and lasting. A new way of doing things; expanded possible actions; learning is now part of being; it is systemic; organizational learning; enthusiasm for change and learning.
3	Shift conversational patterns in positive and productive directions.	The ability to deliver a message independent of interference. The ability to discern and explore assessments, make personal connections and commitments. A line of sight effectively connecting people collectively with end-state outcomes (ie., the finished model plane).
4	Recognize the context and environmental dynamics within which the organization and employees work.	Our ability to improve our outcomes is greatly dependent on the organization's cultural and environmental dynamics. Recognizing those dynamics and understanding the holistic systems within which they operate.
5	Build, sustain and repair trust.	Leaders must be sincere, competent and reliable. The absence of trust at any point renders conversations immobile. Once trust is established it must be renewed persistently.
6	Promote and foster wisdom and confidence.	Creating situations where trust is evident through outcomes. Proven confidence that effective action will take place. Demonstrated confidence in getting and delivering on an agenda, and empowering others through both their collaboration and self-direction.
7	Exhibit leadership presence.	The ability to engage in conversations and deliver messages independent of interference. To powerfully employ body posture, the physical environment as well as powerfully employ emotional connections.

"One of the most common and costly losses in corporate and organizational life is passion," Victor added. "Getting in touch with one's aspirations—or getting back in touch with them—and connecting them to real goals and outcomes, is often what distinguishes a great leader and coach."

As usual, Justine was writing notes as fast as she could.

"And as you know very well by now," Victor continued, "a leader as coach can engage conversations to explore alternative ideas and interpretations, evaluate options, and make well-grounded decisions. A leader as coach supports learning as a skill set that improves performance, satisfaction, and well-being."

Justine sat up in her chair, looking Victor in the eye. Calmly, she said, "I think I am ready for tomorrow."

PART THREE

TAKING FLIGHT

There are in nature neither rewards nor punishments, there are consequences.

—Robert Ingersoll

In the arena of human life the honors and rewards fall to those who show their good qualities in action.

—Aristotle

CHAPTER FIFTEEN

ROYAL MOUNTED CANADIAN POLICE

The Royal Canadian Mounted Police are Canada's national police force, providing law enforcement services in detachments across the country. Affectionately referred to as "Mounties," the Royal Canadian Mounted Police have frequently captured the attention of British and American authors and have appeared in hundreds of novels, stories, and films over the last century, creating a vivid and popular icon of the mounted police as fearless and unfailing.

The red-coated Mountie, with broad-brimmed Stetson hat, is in reality more substance than image. From the beginning of its 125-year history this distinctive unit has served Canadian people by establishing order in the frontier reaches of their vast country. As the population grew, the Mounted Police adapted, continuing to ensure the peace and security of its citizens across the land.

As Justine sat in her office early the next morning, she felt somewhat like a Mountie. She was on a frontier of discord, trying to manage in an arena where every decision could have significant consequences. Nick's presentation to senior management was later that afternoon. Before that, she had a morning staff meeting with her leads, starting in a few minutes, and she was gathering her thoughts.

On her way to meet with her leads, Justine paused briefly to review the process metrics on the business dashboard posted outside her office. She couldn't help but wonder whether any communication and conversational metrics should be represented. "If organizations are networks of conversations," she thought, "why aren't we monitoring the network?"

Justine was the first to arrive for the meeting, and instead of taking her usual seat at the head of the table, she intentionally took a place near the center of one of the table's sides. When Fran came in, she sat next to Justine. Matt took a place across the table. Lester sat at the end of the table.

"Did you hear it's supposed to rain this afternoon?" Matt said as he sat down.

"No, I didn't," responded Justine. "And my umbrella's in the car. I'll have to go get it later."

Fran seemed agitated, and didn't have time for casual chat. "Do you know what's going on?" she asked Justine directly. "I know you probably have things you want to cover, but I heard there's a big meeting this afternoon."

"I heard the same thing," Lester added. "Nick's pulled a coup."

"You know, I am glad you brought that up," Justine replied, assuredly. "That was actually my first agenda topic. I want to let you all know everything I know, and take it from there, OK?"

All heads nodded.

"We've all been working hard on the SciTech proposal, which is due in two weeks. Since SciTech is in our region, but clearly has worldwide impact, we have been working together with Nick, Nora, and Sean, as well as others in product development and marketing. We have also certainly heard from Harvey that concerns exist regarding our progress and about what we have been able to show senior management thus far."

Heads nodded again.

Justine paused, slowing her voice slightly as she spoke again. "Yesterday morning I found out from Harvey that Nick scheduled a meeting with senior management to review his team's proposal for SciTech. I did not know about the meeting before yesterday. I asked to be included in the meeting and Harvey said fine."

Justine saw the looks of disappointment begin to set in. "Let me add two other things," she quickly continued. "First, I am not going to let the fabulous work done here, by this team," she opened her hands and gestured to each person, "go unaccounted for. I am not simply going this afternoon to sit and listen. I am going to discuss our solution in what I think is a unique way."

"What exactly do you mean," Lester asked.

"Lester," Justine responded, "You have done some amazing work on projecting product modifications to meet SciTech's stated goals. But you've gone further than that, too—you have extrapolated your assessment of their future needs and looked at fundamental ways in which we could improve our production process to meet them."

Lester sat up in his chair and put his hands on the table.

Justine looked around the table. She considered standing up, and then decided to roll back her chair a bit so that she could motion with her arms more visibly.

"Please know this," Justine told her colleagues. "The first thing is that we have been following a very good strategy, contributing our effort, knowledge and skills, leveraging increasingly collaborative team dynamics, and using feedback from anyone who would talk with us to guide and shape our deliverable."

Justine saw smiles begin to creep onto her leads' faces. She could tell that her declaration was infusing positive energy into everyone in the room.

"Here's the second thing," Justine continued. "I am convinced that as a result of our work on behalf of this prospect, we are extremely well-positioned to deliver an outcome acceptable to all stakeholders. And along the way, we are improving our individual and team effectiveness, improving our individual and team satisfaction, and very importantly, improving the future capability of our team."

Justine could clearly feel the enthusiasm in the room. She continued with her additional agenda topics and let the team know that she would circle back with them later in the afternoon, after the big meeting. She also let them know that she was going to visit with Nick shortly. After that, there was good dialogue on a number of other topics. Each lead contributed meaningfully to the conversation, and when it was time to adjourn, Justine let the leads wrap things up.

As her team filed out of the room after the meeting, Justine felt proud. She had been able to make shifts, and influence the conversation, in positive and productive ways. But while she was glad that the latest discussion had gone well, she was acutely aware that numerous conversations of significant consequence and magnitude lay directly ahead.

CHAPTER SIXTEEN

PATHS OF RESISTANCE

J ustine glanced out the window as she walked down the corridor toward Nick's office. The sky was a deep gray. In the trees by the parking lot leaves wavered in a gentle breeze.

Alone in his office, Nick was bent over his desk, evidently reviewing material for his presentation. Justine knocked lightly on the doorframe.

"Hi, Nick. Have you got a few minutes?"

"Um, sure," Nick said. "But just a few. I've got a number of things to get to shortly." He started tidying stacks of paper on his desk.

"No problem, this should be quick," Justine said as she sat down.

"So, what's up?" Nick asked, leaning back and rocking slightly in his chair.

Sitting up straight, Justine tried to look Nick in the eyes. "First off, Nick, I wanted to let you know that I talked with Harvey yesterday, and he told me about the presentation this afternoon..."

"Look, Justine," Nick interrupted, "we have all been feeling the pressure and when my team crossed a finish line in our work, to a point where we're ready to go to senior management, I simply told Harvey we were ready." Nick glanced at Justine, then looked out the door and around the room a bit. "It's nothing against you guys."

"I'm sure," Justine continued, nodding. "My assessment is that you have been working as quickly as you can to get to a point where you could get in front of senior management, and that's fine."

She took her hand out of her lap and gestured as Nick looked on. "I wanted to also let you that I will be there this afternoon, and plan to introduce aspects of the proposal we have all been working on, one which your team has certainly contributed to."

"Senior management has no appetite for competing proposals, if that's what you're aiming for," Nick replied, picking up a pen and tapping it on his desktop.

Justine edged closer to Nick's desk. "I am not intending to compete, Nick. We are on the same team. I do think, though, that there may be additional elements of value, other possibilities, to share with senior management."

"Look, my team and I have been through this before," Nick responded. "We have the experience SPI needs at a time like this. We'll show that this afternoon."

"Perhaps," Justine said, smiling gently. "Well, I'd be happy to discuss or share more with you if you are interested."

"No, I think I'm all set. And I pretty pushed for time at this point," Nick said. He tapped his computer keyboard to turn off his screen-saver.

"O.K. then," Justine replied, nodding at Nick as she got up to leave. "See you this afternoon." Nick barely glanced at her before he made a point of turning back to his papers.

Walking back to her office, Justine remembered one of the take-away items Victor had given her after one of their coaching conversations, about the fact that there are always impediments to improving conversations. Victor had given her another of his trademark laminated cards. This one listed the "Top 10 Prominent Derailers" of conversational capability.

Back in her office, Justine pulled that card from her attaché and reviewed its contents. She identified with it more now than when she was first introduced to it.

	Conversational Capacity	
	Top 10 Prominent Derailers	

#	Derailer	Description
1	Arrogance	Reluctance to admit that we do not know something or another can teach us.
2	Complacent	"Given the way that I am, I cannot change!"
3	Helpless	"I don't know, and what I don't know can't be changed!"
4	Unimportant	"I haven't got time, I'm too busy!"
5	Triviality	Reluctant to take learning seriously.
6	Barriers	Inability and/or unwillingness to unlearn old ways.
7	Incomplete	Overlooking the mood/emotional context, the body/physical presence.
8	Ineffective	Confusing learning with acquiring information (information does not equal wisdom).
9	Mistrusting	Unwilling to genuinely learn from others, lack of faith in broader objectives.
10	Impatience	Satisfaction with superficial versus lasting results.

Justine placed the card on her desk, leaning it against the corner of her computer. She began to think that the coaching world in which Victor operated and her corporate world were coming into convergence. Or were they headed for a collision?

CHAPTER SEVENTEEN

DISTINCTIONS

Eating lunch at her desk, Justine recalled how dinner at home the night before had reminded her of another of Victor's notions, this one about "building distinctions." Sipping a glass of wine with her husband, Justine observed that while she and Fred enjoyed the occasional glass of wine, they hardly considered themselves connoisseurs. There are wine enthusiasts who basically pour and drink, Justine knew, just as there are those who buy wine with great care, knowing what they like and which wine goes with which type of food. And then, of course, there are the true aficionados who treat wine as more an art form than a beverage.

Victor's point, which he labeled the "concept of distinctions," was that different people perceive things differently based on their existing predispositions. Victor used the simple example of the stars in the sky. Some people just see white dots, he said, while others see constellations and astronomical features. Still others still see zodiac signs and astrological items. The bottom line, Victor said, is that we all see through the lenses of our knowledge, experiences, and predispositions.

"To distinguish is to make one part of the whole stand out from the rest," Victor had said. "Distinctions highlight or bring into our view particular objects, individuals, properties or actions. Each person perceives conversations in a different light. The more distinctions we have with language, emotions, and physicality, the more capable we are to navigate conversations effectively."

After she finished her sandwich, Justine slipped out to pick up her umbrella in case it rained later. She was closing her car's trunk when she was startled to see Guy McNamara, SPI's CEO, walking nearby.

She paused for a moment. As Guy came closer he slowed and then stopped as he and Justine made eye contact.

"Mr. McNamara, hello," Justine said, a little taken aback.

Guy smiled warmly and shook Justine's hand. She immediately noticed that their handshake was not quick and rigid, but yielding and unhurried.

"Justine Fullerton, glad to bump into you," Guy said. "Please call me Guy. I'm just on my way in from a meeting offsite."

"I was just grabbing my umbrella," replied Justine. Justine suspected that the CEO would be part of the afternoon's meeting, and she decided to use their chance encounter as an opportunity to ask him about SciTech. She knew that she would have to act fast, since the busy man was about to slip away.

"If you don't mind me asking," she said, "what's your perspective on the SciTech prospect?"

"It's certainly a big, exciting opportunity for us," Guy replied as they walked together toward the front door. "We'll need to put our best foot forward as a company."

Keeping pace with Guy's rapid steps, Justine said, "I agree. I think there are some huge possibilities for us."

"Possibilities," Guy repeated, as they walked into SPI's lobby. "That's a good word for it. I'm interested in seeing what's in store. It was nice to see you. Take care." He waved and turned down the hallway toward the executive offices.

"Thanks," Justine replied. "You too." She squeezed the handle of her umbrella and turned quickly toward her office. She hadn't felt this sure of herself in a long time. She felt, in fact, like she might be learning to read the stars.

CHAPTER EIGHTEEN

MOMENTS OF TRUTH

With its state-of-the-art lighting and sound systems, digital videoconferencing services, integrated presentation screens, and other technological accoutrements, the executive conference room at SPI was a showcase. For Nick's proposal on SciTech, the room had been reserved weeks in advance by Harvey Mumford, one of only a handful of executives who had the right to reserve the much-desired space.

Nick was in the middle of his presentation now. Justine watched him present slides that outlined a strategy for how best to respond to SciTech. Nick was polished, as usual. He outlined SciTech's product needs, showed how SPI's suggested product offering could match those needs, and proposed a slew of convincing approaches to accomplish the task. From his demeanor down to details like his choice of clothing, his performance was seamless and flawless. Except that it wasn't. Not to Justine.

She listened to Nick, to the executives around the room who were mostly silent during the presentation. She listened to Guy, the CEO. When Nick finished, he thanked everyone for their time and asked for questions. A few executives asked for clarification of particular details. Justine sat on the edge of her seat as the sparse dialogue pinged around the room, like a slow moving pinball bouncing softly off a bumper, heading towards an awaiting flipper.

After a moment, Guy McNamara—Justine's hunch that he would attend was right—asked if there were any other questions or comments. Justine, already leaning up from her chair, raised her hand.

"Justine Fullerton, please go ahead," invited Guy.

"Thank you," Justine started. She felt all of the sudden flushed, recognizing that all eyes were on her. "Let me first say what a great presentation by Nick." She could see that Nick was looking directly at her and could tell that he was intensely curious about what she would say next.

"I know a lot of work went into it," Justine continued, "by both Nick's team, my team, and others at SPI." In his presentation, Nick had failed to acknowledge the role of his team, Justine's team, or any other supporting department.

"My question has to do with the possibilities we are addressing in our proposal," Justine went on, looking at individuals to begin gauging their reactions. Seeing eyes begin to wander she continued, "My assessment of the direction represented here thus far is that while it certainly meets SciTech's expressed needs today, and is highly product-focused, we have the opportunity to go in a different, albeit related direction."

"Tell us what you mean," Guy asked, still looking at Justine.

"SciTech is the most significant opportunity for SPI in some time," Justine stated. "And as such I think we have the opportunity to lead not with the product, but the relationship."

At the front of the room, Nick began to shake his head— whether in disagreement or disappointment, Justine couldn't be sure.

"Relationships are built on trust," Justine persisted. "And I would offer that trust is made of reliability, sincerity, and competence. SPI has proven for over 30 years that we can make products that work. Our reliability is not in question. Given that, I think our focus could shift to sincerity and competence."

The room was quiet, and while Justine couldn't gauge the reaction to what she was saying, she clearly had everyone's attention. She looked around the room and tried to make eye contact as she talked.

"To be very specific, I would lead with the relationship, with building a trusting communication with SciTech, emphasizing our sincerity to do business honestly. I would stress our competence by addressing not only what was included in their documentation, but by representing our ability to grow with them. Lester Fowler and others have done some incredible work to predict SciTech's future product needs, and while those ideas are not formally incorporated into the proposal, I would suggest working them in."

Numerous heads began to nod, and a slight murmur started as a few attendees shifted in their seats. Justine heard someone whisper, "She's on to something."

"In conclusion," Justine said, sensing her time expiring, "I firmly believe there is slightly different approach that would give us an improved opportunity to build a collaborative future with SciTech, one that is as rich in possibilities for us as it is economically viable. I'd be happy to discuss it more at any time."

"Thanks for your comment, Justine," Guy stated, as the murmuring grew louder. "Are there any more comments?" The room briefly quieted. "OK, thanks everyone,", and Guy adjourned the meeting. As executives quickly gathered their things and began to depart, Justine slowly rose from her chair. She caught a penetrating glare from Nick before he bolted out the door. Guy McNamara nodded subtly to her as he left the room.

On the way back to her office, Justine thought about the story of the pebbles and the girl standing on the pebble-strewn path.

She thought about choices and possibilities, about having the courage to try something uncommon, and about the reality of unforeseen consequences.

And while she was privately pleased with her own remarks, Justine took even more satisfaction from knowing that she had used her platform in the meeting to acknowledge her team's work. Justine didn't know it at the time, but she would not have to wait long before the consequences of her action would begin to unfold.

CONVERSATION INNOVATION

CHAPTER NINETEEN

TWO RIGHTS AND A WRONG

ater that afternoon Justine was reading email in her office when heard a knock at her door. She looked up and saw Nick standing in her doorway.

"Nick, hi, come on in," Justine said. She was a little surprised to see him; Nick rarely visited other people's work areas.

Nick looked uncomfortable. He fidgeted by the doorway, scanning the room, taking in the family photographs that decorated Justine's desk.

"Have a seat, Nick," Justine said. "What's up?"

Nick got right to the point. "Listen," he said, "I am not sure what kind of stunt you were trying to pull earlier at the SciTech meeting, but it's going to backfire on both of us."

"I'm not sure what you mean, Nick," Justine replied. There was an awkward pause of silence as Nick looked around.

"I know you haven't been in management too long," Nick started again, "but what happened back there is not how things get done." Nick looked directly at Justine. She could feel how upset he was. "Harvey was fine with the plan, although he obviously disappeared at the end. And I can't figure out why you'd interfere like that."

"Nick, my comments had nothing to do with you personally. My assessment was, and is, that there may be another way to approach SciTech. Too much good work has been going on not to allow other alternative considerations to reach the right audiences."

"The right audiences! That was my meeting!" Nick exclaimed. "I have been patiently keeping you and your team in the loop, but when it's time for action I can't see why you got involved."

"Let me say a couple things, Nick," Justine said, working hard to keep her tone calm. "First of all, it shouldn't matter how long I've been at SPI or been a manager here. There's no right or wrong in that. Second, we may have a sincere difference of opinion about how to structure the SciTech deal. There's nothing wrong with that. In fact, as a company those differences should make us stronger, if we let them."

Nick was slowly shaking his head. Justine intended to finish her train of thought out loud even though her perception was that Nick was no longer listening.

"Third and last, and this is very pertinent even right now, is that our discussing or having a conversation about alternative solutions or possibilities is critically important for us as a business and us as a management team."

"You made it personal, Justine," Nick interjected. "Everyone could see that."

"I don't think so, Nick," Justine quickly countered. "There is no personal agenda or outcome on my part. I honestly appreciate the work you and your team have done. I just had other suggestions which I felt should have been aired."

"At whose expense?" Nick asked. He stood up and motioned to leave.

"Nick," Justine stood and tried to catch his eye as he turned, "what I said about trust in the meeting is just as applicable inside SPI as it is between SPI and its biggest clients."

"Meaning what?" Nick turned to face Justine. "Everybody knows about trust. I'm really not sure how it's even relevant here."

"For one thing," Justine replied, "trusting too little is just as detrimental as trusting too much. We are on the same team, Nick."

"I've got to run, Justine." With that, Nick walked out the door. Justine thought about following him, but remained standing in her office for a few moments. She sat down calmly and hit the button to refresh her email. She tried to re-focus her thinking toward other tasks on her to-do list.

Sometimes certain things work out and others don't, she told herself. She knew the impact a negative mood could cause, and chose instead to focus on the positives of the day, and on the excitement that accompanied the uncertainties still ahead.

CHAPTER TWENTY

LIMITS AND POSSIBILITIES

It was well after five that afternoon when Justine again heard a knock at her door. It was Fran. She was smiling broadly.

"Fran, please come in," Justine called out cordially. She was pleased to get an unannounced visit from one of her leads.

"Do you have time now?" asked Fran, stepping cautiously into Justine's office. "I can come back tomorrow."

"Yes, now is fine," Justine reassured her. "I was just finishing up some busy work. I am delighted to see you. What's up?"

"Well, first off I wanted to congratulate you!" Fran stated as she sat down.

"Congratulate?" Justine repeated, "For what?"

"We all heard about the big meeting earlier this afternoon. We heard about what you said." Fran was nodding her head and smiling. "Justine, we're so excited for you—and for us, too. This is so great!"

Justine was still not clear on what exactly Fran was referring to. She was about to ask when the phone rang. She looked at the phone's internal caller ID display and saw that it was Guy McNamara.

"Fran, I'd like to continue this conversation," Justine said, "but it looks like the CEO is calling me. I should probably take this."

"I'll be back in a few minutes, then?" suggested Fran.

"That would be great. Sorry, and thank you," replied Justine. As Fran scooted out of her office, Justine immediately picked up the phone before its next ring.

"This is Justine Fullerton."

"Justine, this is Guy McNamara. Glad I caught you."

Justine stared at the wall above her phone, pressing the handset closer to her ear.

"Mr. McNamara, hello, how are you?" Justine stammered.

"Good, good. Listen, your comments in today's SciTech session really hit the mark. If the work is there as you say, which I'm sure it is, I think we may have found our way. I appreciate all that you and your team have put into this."

"And Nick's team as well," Justine replied, "along with product development and marketing. It really was a team effort."

"I know it was," Guy replied. "Look, as you know we have to go out there to pitch this thing week after next. I'll have my assistant forward the details to you. I'm looking forward to it."

"Thank you, so am I," Justine responded. She was stunned.

"Take care, Justine. I'll be seeing you," Guy said before signing off the call.

Justine felt like screaming for joy and laughing out loud, all at the same time. She called Fran, who raced back to Justine's office. Justine's beaming smile confirmed Fran's suspicions. "I knew it!" Fran said. "I knew he was going to call. SciTech's your deal now! Way to go!"

"Whoa, Fran," Justine interrupted. "This is our deal. You, Lester, Matt, even Sean and Nora, all made this happen. I was fortunate to be able to have the conversation."

"Well, from what I heard, you were full of energy and passion," Fran continued.

Buoyed by the excitement they shared, Fran and Justine continued chatting for nearly an hour, even though they had both been there since very early in the day. The enthusiasm was nice to be a part of. Justine told Fran that her motivation was as much learning as it was working. Justine shared her 'recipe for enthusiastic learning', which she had created on a 3x5 index card as a small tribute to Victor.

	Justine's Recipe for Enthusiastic Learning
#	**Description**
1	Create an "I Want" List—Write down 15 things you want in your life now.
2	Create a "To Do" List—Write down 15 actions which should be completed.
3	Create a "To Be" List—Write down 15 traits you would like to embody.
4	Ask great questions.
5	Determine when and where your mood is naturally at its best.
6	Spend time helping others—give of yourself.
7	Take into account current and historical role models you associate with.
8	Allow yourself time and space to pursue both what you must do pragmatically and what you wish to do passionately.
9	Stimulate your intuition and feed your wisdom.
10	Work just as hard to do something which brings heartfelt joy, fun and laughter (to yourself and others).

CHAPTER TWENTY-ONE

MIRRORS

The sleek, modern lobby at SciTech was perfectly suited to a successful global organization. Elegant maps illustrating SciTech offices around the world hung from the walls. Enlarged excerpts from corporate communication pieces depicted SciTech's senior leaders. Etched in glass, the company's mission, vision statement, and commitment to shareholders were on prominent display.

Justine waited in the lobby with Guy McNamara and SPI's SciTech relationship team. They were about to present their RFP response to SciTech's senior leadership group.

In the few moments they had prior to going into the meeting, Justine looked around the reception area. She thought back to the diversity seminar she attended a few months ago. She thought about her visits with Victor and their coaching conversations.

Studying the pictures of SciTech employees on the walls, she wondered, how many 'Justines' work at SciTech? How many new managers are looking for their way? How many of them are fortunate enough to find it?

How many Nicks are there? How many Harveys? And what about the Lesters, Frans, and Matts, or Seans and Noras? How do they get along?

Justine clutched the handle on her attaché case. A door opened behind the security desk and her team was ushered inside. Justine smiled and stepped into her next conversation.

EPILOGUE

LIFE GOES ON

In the months and years that followed, Justine continued to develop her conversational capabilities. She continued to meet with Victor periodically, and began to apply coaching in her own right. Select individuals at SPI and elsewhere sought her out for advice and counsel, and she was more than happy to share her insights.

Over time, Justine also broadened her use of powerful conversations to her home life, volunteer work, and other activities outside of SPI.

Her own responsibilities grew quickly. SPI received the SciTech contract, which turned out to be the first of many in a productive new relationship, and Justine added new leads to her team to support that work. Later, she was the first in management to take responsibility for a large district territory made up of a group of regions.

Justine felt that SPI turned a milestone corner as a result of its work with SciTech. Over time, she noticed, the culture at SPI became more collaborative, more accommodating and supportive of genuine debate, and more patient with and receptive to possibilities. To be sure, it wasn't always rosy: some staff at SPI continued to work differently in meetings than one-on-one, there were constant reminders that people use significantly different learning styles to solve problems, and some colleagues simply resisted any efforts to change SPI. But overall, conversations across the company became increasingly more open, effective, and productive.

Weathering business changes, adjusting to different bosses, and dealing with occasional inter-office struggles, Justine maintained a focus on what she believed to be truly important: trust, learning, and being as effective as she could through language, emotions and mood, and physical presence.

As an ever-present symbol of her story, Justine placed a black pebble in a small glass jar on her desk. It reminded her of the power of conversations, and about how much she still had to learn, and about the importance of her enduring journey.

APPENDIX

METHODS

It is important that an aim never be defined in terms of activity or methods. It must always relate directly to how life is better for everyone.

—W. Edwards Deming

By three methods we may learn wisdom: First, by reflection, which is noblest; second, by imitation, which is easiest; and third by experience, which is the bitterest.

—Confucius

What is Ontology and Ontological Coaching?

Ontology comes from the branch of metaphysics that deals with the nature of being. In philosophy, ontology (from the Greek ont: of being, and ology: science, study, theory) is the most fundamental branch of metaphysics. It studies being or existence and their basic categories and relationships, to determine what entities and what types of entities exist. Ontology therefore has strong implications for conceptions of reality.

Schools of thought aligned with subjectivism, objectivism, and relativism have existed throughout the 20th century, while postmodernists have endeavored to reframe many of their key questions into terms of 'beings taking some specific action in an environment'. This work relied to a great extent on insights derived from scientific research into animals taking instinctive action in natural and artificial settings, as studied by biology and the cognitive sciences.

The word "ontology" means study of being. Ontological coaching is about coaching to a way of being, as a means of producing major shifts in perception and behavior. In ontological coaching, way of being is regarded as the driving influence of behavior. Performance and effectiveness are shaped by one's way of being.

Way of being is represented by three interrelated domains of human existence. These three domains are language, emotions, and physiology (body posture). Our way of being can be thought of as the internal reality we live within, which especially includes the relationship we have with ourselves. It is from this internal reality that we form our perceptions about the external world and how we participate in it.

In the late 20th century, advances in philosophy and biology produced major developments in functionally understanding the power of language and communication. These breakthroughs formed the foundational methodology of ontological coaching.

The ontological coaching methodology contains a set of tools and techniques for observing and shifting ways of being. These tools and techniques can generally be applied through:

- Linguistic acts
- Emotions and moods
- Body posture and physical presence
- Listening
- The power of conversations
- The role of stories and narratives
- Holding the coachee (or protégé) as a legitimate other
- Identifying the breakdown and/or the key issues for coaching

Much of the recent work driving ontology and ontological coaching comes from the work of Humberto Maturana and Rafael Echeverria. Maturana's work explores and expands the notion of "the observer": As humans we are observers of the world and, as such, we are living systems who live in language and through language make interpretations about how the world is for us. Rafael Echeverria is one of the key developers of the "ontological approach." Echeverria originally outlined the approach and set of distinctions which were developed by Fernando Flores, Echeverria himself, and Julio Olalla in The Ontology of Language.

How does coaching work?

Coaching is a professional relationship that enhances the coachee's ability to effectively focus on learning, make changes, achieve desired goals, and experience fulfillment. Ontological coaching can be described as the studied use and understanding of language, moods and physicality for effective learning and change. Ontological coaching reveals and challenges 'the way things are' and 'the ways they have tended to stay the same' for individuals and organizations, and opens up entirely novel yet well-worn avenues to change so that desired results can be created.

This simple model shows how ontological coaching works:

OBSERVER ⟶ ACTION ⟶ RESULT

In the work of organizations and individuals within them, a shared understanding (relying on a common understanding of meaning) leads to coordination of action, which in turn leads to desired outcomes (represented in the simple model above). If an action is changed, results will surely change. When shifts as an observer are made, a new range of possible actions are generated, opening up a whole new set of possible results.

Different from typical performance feedback and coaching, ontological coaching (built off its 'way of being' foundation) occurs at the level of the observer and gets to the root of perception and reality to foster real, lasting, positive change.

Examples of relevant ontological questions include:

• Am I separating assessments from assertions?
• What's going on with me?
• What interpretation am I living in?
• How well is this interpretation serving me?
• How come I am observing things in this way?
• Just exactly how am I languaging this situation to myself?
• What is happening with me emotionally and bodily?
• What shifts in language, emotions, and body will be important?
• How am I formulating reality?
• Is this conversation generating shared meaning?
• How am I listening right now?
• What am I listening to?
• Where am I listening from?
• How might my prejudices be interfering with my listening?
• How do these interpretations impact my emotions?
• How could I shift my body to listen differently?
• Am I holding the other person as a legitimate other?
• What predispositions are helping/challenging this situation?
• What assessments/meta-assessments are at work in this conversation?

What is an ontological coach?

An ontological coach is a particular kind of professional coach. An ontological coach is one who is able to observe how individuals construct interpretations about their existence, which are reflected through their emotions, body, use of language, and elsewhere.

Through conversations, an ontological coach is able to assist others in becoming aware of the interpretations through which they construct their perceptions and how these can be changed. An ontological coach has the capacity to work across the diverse domains of human realities, addressing personal and professional concerns. An ontological coach is a professional who possesses powerful ontological distinctions.

An ontological coach can open up powerful new areas of learning that produce deep change, enabling people to function more effectively and creatively, and to succeed in the midst of a turbulent world, specifically:

- Enhancing the quality of our public and private conversations.
- Enabling us to develop more constructive interpretations that expand what is possible for us in the quality of our relationships.
- Generating realities that open more possibilities for our engagement in life.
- Improving the quality of our behavior and communication.
- Producing more positive results (especially in conversations/ relationships).
- Enhancing the overall quality of our existence.

Questions for Review and Discussion

Introduction
- Do you think people "babble?"
- Do you believe that when individuals communicate clearly, challenging tasks are surmountable?
- What examples can you think of where an effort failed due to lack of effective communication/conversations?
- Do you believe you are open to the learning inherent in this book?

Chapter 1
- Have you ever attended a "diversity" seminar?
- Do you have any experience with coaching?
- What do you think of the definition and description (bullet points) of coaching?
- What did you think of the parable?

Chapter 2
- How demanding is your work environment?
- How long do you generally retain knowledge from seminars?
- What impact do corporate programs (Six Sigma, business dashboards) have on conversations?
- How many confidants do you have in the workplace?
- What's the culture at SPI like? How does it compare to your organization?

Chapter 3
- What are staff meetings and status meeting like for you?
- Is there active conversation and discussion on the right topics?
- Is there gossip? Is it more of a positive, a nuisance, or detrimental to productivity?
- Is everyone on the same page with regard to outcomes?
- What do you think of how Justine handled her meeting?

Chapter 4
- Are you ever surprised by something at work?
- What do you make of Justine's reaction to the news?
- What do you think of Nick and Justine's relationship at this point?
- What is your opinion about 'inside/outside the box' thinking? Can you point to specific examples of its relevance?

Chapter 5
- How do you think Justine handles herself in these brief 1-1s?
- What do you think of the different dynamics inherent in 1-1 versus in the meeting room?
- Is Justine relating well to each individual?
- Should she have interrupted Lester?
- Do you think her faith in her team is well placed?

Chapter 6
- How important is "rapport" for a team? Is it like "chemistry" on sports teams?
- Are there important cultural distinctions between employees more recently hired from outside companies and longer-tenured employees?
- Where do you think Nick is coming from? What is his agenda and motivation?
- What kind of conversation were Nick and Justine having?

Chapter 7
- What would you have done if you were Justine?
- Should she have gone to her boss immediately?
- Was she right to call Victor?

Chapter 8
- How important is it that a CEO be personable?
- How much influence does an organization's top executive really have?
- How important is middle management?
- Do you think executives are like royalty? In what ways would you say they are and in which ways would you say they aren't?

Part One

• Do people tend to remain in their "comfort zone?"
• Is it necessary to step outside that zone to be successful?
• What happened to Justine to cause a shift?
• What awareness and motivation is in play?
• At this point, how would you characterize Justine and her performance?
• What, if anything, did you learn thus far?

Chapter 10

• Is Justine a good listener?
• Do you agree with the types of speech acts noted?
• Can you give examples of each from your own experience?
• What is the link between speech act or language and results? How is the link established and maintained?

Chapter 11

• What is the mood in Justine's team at this point?
• What is the mood in Nick's team at this point?
• What is the mood in Justine's discussions with Victor?
• What is the mood in your immediate environment? In your organization?
• What is the impact of one person's negative moods/emotions on others?
• What is the impact of one person's positive moods/emotions on others?
• Are moods/emotions contagious? Can you give examples?

Chapter 12

• Is "body language" a real thing?
• What are the positive and negative impacts of physical presence?
• Is physical presence innate or can it be controlled?
• Is physical presence/body physiology a personal, organizational, and/or cultural characteristic?

Chapter 13

- Can a feasible whole be made from infeasible parts?
- When is a team less than the sum of its parts?
- What role do outside influences playing in Justine's work life?
- What role do outside influences play in your everyday work life?
- Is the notion of the whole relevant in the work of individuals in organizations today?

Chapter 14

- What breakdowns does Justine experience to this point?
- What other breakdowns exist in her work or yours?
- What do you think of the leadership traits?
- Are any of them not relevant? Are any more relevant than others?

Part Two

- Is Justine enhancing her capabilities as a manager?
- Are her conversations with Victor effective?
- How realistic are the coaching conversation topics?
- What actions, reactions and lack-of-actions is Justine recognizing?
- At this point, how would you characterize Justine and her performance?
- What, if anything, did you learn thus far?

Chapter 15

- Why aren't organizations monitoring their conversational networks?
- How would you characterize the meeting in terms of language, body and emotions?
- What did Justine do well? What could she have done better?
- What parallels can be drawn to your environment?

Chapter 16

- What kind of conversation did Nick and Justine have?
- What role, if any, did emotions play in the interaction?
- What role, if any, did predispositions play in the conversation?
- How effective was Nick? How effective was Justine?
- What is your opinion of the "derailers?"

Chapter 17

• What impact do you think distinctions play at work?
• Can you think of other examples of useful distinctions?
• How would you characterize Justine's conversation with Guy in terms of language, body and emotions?
• Given what you know, what do you think Guy's perception of the conversation was?

Chapter 18

• What do you think of the meeting? Was it a good meeting?
• Do meetings like this occur in your organization?
• What do you think of what Justine said? How she said it?
• What do you think of Guy's comments?
• What would you have done if you were in the room?

Chapter 19

• Where do you think Nick was coming from? What was his perception? What do you think of it?
• How often do you think these kinds of conversations occur at SPI?
• How often do you think these kinds of conversations occur at your organization?
• Do you think trusting too little is just as detrimental as trusting too much? How and why?
• How did Justine handle herself? What would you have done/not done?

Chapter 20

• What do you think of what Fran was doing?
• How do you think Justine handled the conversation with Fran?
• How do you think Justine handled the conversation with Guy?
• What do you think of Justine's "recipe for enthusiastic learning?"
• What do you think of her sharing it?

Chapter 21

• How do you think Justine prepared for the meeting?
• What do you think will happen in the meeting with SciTech?

Part Three

- What, if any, enhanced capabilities has Justine brought to SPI?
- What application of new distinctions has Justine exhibited?
- What were the implications—positive and negative?
- At this point, how would you characterize Justine and her performance?
- What, if anything, did you learn?

Additional Questions

- What barriers did Justine experience? How did she deal with them?
- Are some individuals really different in 1-1 conversations versus in group settings? Why? What can/should be done about it?
- What other advice or coaching would you have offered Justine? At what point?
- What advice or coaching would you offer Nick?
- How could Victor have been more effective?
- What do you think Guy would think about coaching?
- What do you think Harvey would think about coaching?
- What impact do you think Justine will have as a boss? With a larger team?
- What role do bosses (and specifically conversations with one's boss) play in employee performance?
- Is it true that 70-90% of what people "hear" is non-verbal? If so, what's being done about it?
- How could conversational capabilities be monitored on business dashboards? In other ways?
- How long do you think Justine will retain what she has learned?
- What other questions do you have?

Structured Team Discussion—Example

This general outline is offered as a means to enhance the value individuals and teams can gain from the learning experience.

This is an example of a series of Team and Individual activities. See the **Additional Resources** section for more information.

Stage	Activities	Duration
Pre-work	All team members read *Conversation Innovation*	Distribute 1-2 weeks prior
	Schedule debrief session	2-4 hours in length
	Send Conversational Capability Baseline Survey to team (if desired)	Complete 1-2 weeks prior
	Enlist facilitator (if desired, or have someone designated as facilitator)	2-4 hours prep time
Team Discussion Session	General debrief on story	20-30 minutes
	Review 10 key discussion questions as a group	30-45 minutes
	Review survey results and normative comparisons (if desired)	30-45 minutes
	Assign each person to select 3 similarities and 3 dissimilarities	15 minutes to think about it, 10 minutes each to discuss with group
	Assign each person to select 3 action steps for themselves and 3 they would like others to take	15 minutes to think about it, 10 minutes each to discuss with group (includes request for coaching)
	Schedule follow-up session in 60 days (if desired)	
Follow-up Session	Review status/progress on action items	45 minutes

Conversational Dynamics Model

The Conversational Dynamics Model represents a holistic approach to improving conversations and network of conversations for individuals, teams, departments, divisions, entire organizations and across value chains.

It recognizes conversational typology, speech acts, private and public conversations, and the impact of language, emotions/moods, and body physiology.

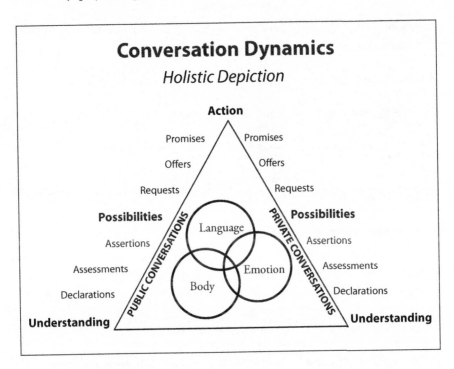

Typical Breakdowns

Breakdowns are a normal, natural part of interaction and represent important learning opportunities. The following is a sample inventory of familiar and unfamiliar breakdowns, typical causes and remedies (there could be multiple Causes for an Indication and vice versa).

See the **Additional Resources** section for more information.

Performance Improvement Opportunities *Prominent Breakdowns*		
Indication...	**Possible Causes Include...**	**Consider Remedy...**
Discord between boss and staff	Distinguishing assessments from assertions	Performance Management
Discord between staff and peers	Slippery promises	Surveys / Questionnaires
Lack of execution and implementation	Unclear conditions of satisfaction	Dashboards / Scorecards
Too much complacency	Lack of shared meaning	Simulations
Too much consensus	Discord among conversation types	Studies
Unproductive conflict	Foggy requests	Training / Education Materials
Lack of respect and support of diverse ideas	Vague offers	Methodologies
Listening challenges	Absence of reliability, sincerity, competence	Document Templates
Lack of self-awareness	Improper use of ungrounded assessments	Standards and Guidelines
Questionable decision-making	Insufficient use of inquiry and exploration	Coaching
Challenges translating plans into results	Prevailing mood of acknowledgement or resentment	Executive management seminar
More...	More...	More...

Additional Resources

Looking for a place to go with questions and or for help?

Interested in assessments, surveys, simulations (both SPI-based and non-SPI-based), etc.?

Would you like to get started with a coach or in coaching?

For more information contact the author at:

David Henkin
david.henkin@villanova.edu

Acknowledgements

Like most worthy outcomes, this book would not have been possible without a team effort.

Of course, reserved for my spouse and children are the most cherished accolades. Their familial support, patience, humor and love often turned labor into liberation.

Many colleagues helped contribute to this work. I have been fortunate to work with so many exceptional individuals and teams. Learning experiences both fortuitous and opportunistic have relentlessly followed me (not always declaring themselves clearly at the time!).

For her trusted navigation, expertise, and support, thanks to Liz Henkin. Thanks also to Stephen G. Pelletier for his exceptional editing and advice.

An innovator and continuing inspiration, James Barnes was there from the beginning. His uniqueness will undoubtedly continue to shape great things.

Very special thanks, appreciation, and respect go to Neil Sicherman. Neil became a master coach on the way to becoming a better human being. Fortunately for me our flight patterns overlapped for an important time—and he graciously afforded me some room beneath his wings.

Finally, thank you in advance to the readers who will shape the next installment of this important transformation. Conversation Innovation is gaining momentum. As its supporters (and detractors) continue their march, the fruit of its splendors glide further into reach for more and more people.

CPSIA information can be obtained
at www.ICGtesting.com
Printed in the USA
BVOW10*1422160717

489262BV00002B/30/P